Hermeneutics versus
science?

Hermeneutics Versus Science?

REVISIONS

A Series of Books on Ethics

General Editors:

Stanley Hauerwas and Alasdair MacIntyre

Hermeneutics Versus Science?

Three German Views

Essays by

H.-G. GADAMER, E. K. SPECHT, W. STEGMÜLLER

Translated, Edited, and Introduced by

John M. Connolly and Thomas Keutner

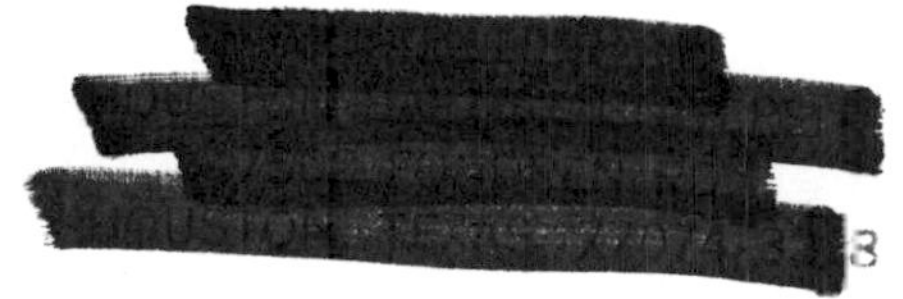

University of Notre Dame Press
Notre Dame, Indiana

Library of Congress Cataloging-in-Publication Data

Hermeneutics versus science?

(Revisions ; v. 8)
Bibliography: p.
Contents: 1. On the circle of understanding / by Hans-Georg Gadamer — 2. Mythopoetic inversion in Rilke's Duino elegies / by Hans-Georg Gadamer — 3. Walther von der Vogelweide's lyric of dream-love and Quasar 3C 273 / by Wolfgang Stegmüller — [etc.]
1. Hermeneutics. 2. Science—Philosophy. 3. Meaning (Philosophy) I. Gadamer, Hans Georg, 1900- . II. Connolly, John M. III. Keutner, Thomas. IV. Specht, E. K. (Ernst Konrad) Literary-critical interpretations—psychoanalytic interpretations. 1988. V. Stegmüller, Wolfgang. Walther von der Vogelweide's lyric of dream-love and Quasar 3C 273. 1988. VI. Series.
BD241.H375 1988 121'.68 87-40346
ISBN 0-268-01084-6
ISBN 0-268-01085-4 (pbk.)

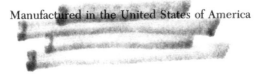

Manufactured in the United States of America

Contents

Acknowledgments

We would like to extend our gratitude, first of all to Professors Gadamer, Specht, and Stegmüller, the authors whose essays we are here publishing; secondly to Professors Hauerwas and MacIntyre, the editors of the Revisions Series; and thirdly to James Langford, Director of the University Press for his cooperation and advice.

Our thanks are also due to the holders of the original copyrights for their permission to publish the translations in this volume:

to Professor Gadamer and J. C. B. Mohr Verlag (Paul Siebeck) in Tübingen for permission to translate and print the first two essays; essay 1 originally appeared as "Vom Zirkel des Verstehens," in: *M. Heidegger zum 70. Geburtstag* , ed. G. Neske, Tübingen 1959; it was reprinted in Gadamer, *Kleine Schriften* IV, Tübingen 1977. Essay 2 made its first appearance in Gadamer, *Kleine Schriften* II, Tübingen 1967 (2nd ed. 1979) under the title "Mythopoietische Umkehrung in Rilke's *Duineser Elegien*";

to the Reclam Verlag, Stuttgart, for permission to publish essay 3. It originally appeared as "Walther von der Vogelweides Lied von der Traumliebe und Quasar 3C 273. Betrachtungen zum sogenannten Zirkel des Verstehens und zur sogenannten Theorienbeladenheit der Beobachtungen" in Stegmüller, *Rationale Rekonstruktion von Wissenschaft und ihrem Wandel*, Stuttgart 1979;

and to Professor Specht for permission to publish essay 4, which first appeared as "Literaturwissenschaftliche Deutungen—Psychoanalytische Deutungen" in *Manuskripte—Zeitschrift für Literatur* 23, June 1984.

Our special thanks go to a number of people who kindly read and commented on the manuscript in whole or part. They are Jan Peter Beckmann, Nikolaus Erichsen, Jay Garfield, Thomas McCarthy, Ernst Konrad Specht, and Ulrich Steinvorth. The Alexander von Humboldt Foundation supported the research which initiated this project, as did various grants for travel and computer resources from Smith College. We also want to express our gratitude for the existence of the BITNET international computer system network, which, by speeding manuscripts back and forth across the Atlantic in hours or even minutes, was an incalculable aid in carrying out this project. And finally we are grateful to Audrey Ryan, Norah Mulvaney, Ann Rice, and Barbara Reed for editorial assistance.

Introduction

Interpretation, Decidability, and Meaning

JOHN M. CONNOLLY AND THOMAS KEUTNER

Is there an art of interpreting which is distinctive of the humanistic disciplines? And is there a special 'act' of understanding which uniquely characterizes those disciplines? These questions concern the status of hermeneutics, which has long been debated in German philosophy. The issue has been revived for contemporary philosophy by the publication of Hans-Georg Gadamer's *Wahrheit und Methode* (*Truth and Method*) in 1960 (English translation 1975), which touched off a lively and wide-ranging debate in which the above-mentioned traditional questions were reformulated. Seen from the standpoint of the new debate, the core of the traditional questions was this: do the hermeneutical disciplines (scriptural exegesis, jurisprudence, literary criticism, history, etc.) differ in some important way from the the natural sciences, i.e., are those disciplines 'autonomous'? Countering claims to the contrary by Hume, Mill, and others, the early champions of the 'autonomy thesis' (Schleiermacher, Ranke, Droysen, et al.) based their position on the alleged independence of the *domain* of the hermeneutical disciplines.[1] Later the thesis was

[1]Hume, Mill, et al. championed what came to be called the 'unity (of science)' thesis. The early history of the 'autonomy-unity' dispute is outlined, with copious references to primary and secondary sources, by Karl-Otto Apel, 1979/1984, Introduction and chaps. I.1 and I.2. As far as possible, we have attempted in this volume to provide page numbers to both the German originals *and* to a readily available English translation.

reformulated to state that the 'disciplines of understanding' distinguish themselves from those of 'explanation' (the sciences of nature) by their *method*, the distinctive mark of which was supposed to lie in a particular 'psychological act', namely understanding. With reference to the the essays collected in this volume we want in this introduction to show, among other things, that today, since Gadamer, the autonomy discussion revolves around the question *whether interpretations in the hermeneutical disciplines are decidable* (i.e., decidably true or false), as is said to be the case with hypotheses in the natural sciences.

It is just this question which is posed by Gadamer's thesis of the 'openness of the text': the interpretation of texts (and in particular 'eminent' texts) can never be regarded as completed. In this sense a valid interpretation does not exclude the validity of other, differing, perhaps even contradictory interpretations. This thesis is argued by Gadamer in the first two essays in this volume, "On the Circle of Understanding"—a preparatory study to his *Wahrheit und Methode*—and "Mythopoetic Inversion in Rilke's *Duino Elegies*."

Especially in the first of these essays Gadamer bases his undecidability thesis on a particular '*ontological*' feature of what has traditionally been called the 'hermeneutical circle' (the view that the meaning of the whole can only be grasped on the basis of the parts, while understanding the meaning of the parts presupposes a grasp of the meaning of the whole). But in essay 3 Wolfgang Stegmüller investigates whether by means of a 'rational reconstruction' the expression 'hermeneutical circle' can in fact, as Wilhelm Dilthey (at the turn of this century) claimed, be construed as marking a method which would distinguish the hermeneutical disciplines from the natural sciences. Stegmüller's search proves futile. As a result, he argues, literary-critical interpretations are to be taken as methodologically equivalent to hypotheses in, say, astronomy

---

Both works are then listed in the Bibliography, while the date of the English edition follows that of the German edition and the page numbers of the two editions are likewise separated by a slash.

or biology, and the autonomy thesis must thus be rejected.

To positivists the thesis of the undecidability of interpretation seems to open the door wide to arbitrariness, for if the hermeneutical canons do not allow us to pick out one interpretation as *the* correct one, then it would appear as though any interpretation is as good as any other. If this were so, hermeneutics would be merely a form of 'the play of the imagination'. The classical concern of positivism is precisely the distinction between what can be confirmed in the confrontation with experience and what is 'merely' subjective. Against the backdrop of this concern, which is by no means limited to positivists, Stegmüller can be viewed as defending the objective character of literary criticism: critics do in fact reject interpretations, and it is the task of the methodologist to say on what rational grounds these rejections are based.[2]

The positions of Gadamer and Stegmüller can, it seems, to some extent be reconciled with one another, a possibility which shows itself in Ernst Konrad Specht's investigations in "Literary-Critical Interpretations—Psychoanalytic Interpretations." On the one hand, Specht contends that one kind of interpretation is straightforwardly decidable. On the other, he makes a case that there are undecidable interpretations which nonetheless can be rationally evaluated On the basis of such evaluation many interpretations are in fact rejected as inadequate without any one interpetation being thereby established as uniquely correct.

In this Introduction we want, first, to show how the conceptual features of interpretation brought to the fore by these differing positions can be, and have been, justified by appeal to precedents in the history of hermeneutics (section 1). Second, we will present an introduction to each of the essays collected in this volume, thereby complementing the historical argument of section 1 with a systematic account of the

[2]Stegmüller, however, does not contend—as did the classical positivists—that the touchstone of such rejection is the confrontation with unvarnished experience.

disputed issues (section 2). We want, finally, to offer the outline of an answer to what we see as the central questions at stake in the debate about decidability here summarized, to wit: whence comes the idea that all interpretations ought to be decidable? and *why* is a certain type of literary interpretation undecidable? The answers we shall propose appeal to the distinction, drawn in recent discussions of the topic of meaning, between truth-conditions and assertability- (or use-) conditions (section 3).

1. Historical Overview

1.1 Interpretation of the Bible

In *Wahrheit und Methode* and elsewhere[3] Gadamer has argued that one of the origins of the thesis that interpretations are decidable was the Reformation controversy concerning the proper interpretation of the Bible. Both of the main parties to that controversy—Catholic and Lutheran—held that scriptural interpretations are in principle decidable, though they differed over the criterion of decidability. This controversy touched off a train of reflection that led, in the work of nineteenth-century theologians, historians, and philosophers, to what Gadamer calls a 'universalization' of the notion of hermeneutics, now conceived as the *method of objective, scientific research in the humanities* (*Geisteswissenschaften*) (section 1.2, below).

Gadamer characterizes the Reformation dispute over the proper interpretation of the Bible as revolving around the question, what does the unique meaning of the Scripture consist in? We want briefly to present Gadamer's view that the thesis that interpretations are decidable was formulated in two different and incompatible ways in the Reformation.

What became at the Council of Trent the official Roman Catholic view held that in the process of interpretation the

[3]E.g., in his Introduction to Gadamer, 1976a, and in his 1972/1982.

tradition of the Church has binding doctrinal authority.[4] If the Church has from the start been protected by the Holy Spirit from substantial error on matters of faith and morals, then it follows that past doctrinal decisions are an unfailing guide for contemporary ones. So it follows also that in matters of scriptural exegesis, themselves of crucial import for doctrinal issues, the testimony of tradition is an indispensable guide.[5]

In this Catholic position we can detect the notion that appeal to tradition allows a later exegete an otherwise unavailable insight into the *intentions* of the Divine and human authors, and that such authorial intention is the criterion of a correct exegesis.[6] There is a familiar procedure in the writing of historical biography which is analogous to the exegetical appeal to tradition. Where the biographer's data include an ambiguous or opaque journal entry made by the subject, now

---

[4]Thus, for example, when the Council defended the traditional interpretation of Jesus' words of Eucharistic institution, it claimed that "these words have their proper and obvious meaning *and were so understood by the Fathers*" (quoted from H. Denziger and A. Schönmetzer, *Enchiridion Symblorum*, Freiburg 1963), cited by R. Brown, in Brown et al., 1968, p. 621.

[5]It was additionally argued, e.g., by Bellarmine (in his *Disputationes* I-III, 1586–1593), that the received text of the Scripture by itself is in fact often so incomplete that, in the absence of the supplementary authority of tradition, its proper interpretation would frequently be doubtful.

[6]The issue is complex because of the purported duality of authorship (and therefore of intention and text-meaning). According to the exegetical practice of a great many Church Fathers and later theologians, the divine intention, particularly in the Old Testament, was at least in part unknown to the human author: "in Hilary's *Tractatus mysteriorum* [ca. 350 A.D.] we find the principle that the Old Testament *in its entirety* is prefigurative of the New Testament," (presumably beyond the intention of the human authors), R. Brown, "Hermeneutics," in R. Brown et al., 1968, p. 612. St. Augustine was equally sweeping. In this notion of human authors unaware of the full meaning of what they write there is an echo of the ancient Greek notion of poetry as 'divinely inspired madness', as well as a foreshadowing of the modern idea that the meaning of the text goes beyond what the author meant by it.

long dead, the biographer cannot of course simply ask the subject what he or she meant. It is, however, possible to try to infer the meaning from external evidence. Of particular value would be information about the subject's authorial intention recorded in letters or diaries by the subject's own family members and passed on from generation to generation. Such information can sometimes constitute decisive support in favor of an interpretive biographical hypothesis.[7] And how much more trust would one have in such information if one believed its transmission to be protected by the Holy Spirit! Thus the Catholic view that the divine intention—mediated by the tradition and protected by the Holy Spirit—constitutes the true meaning of the scriptural text is an early version of the 'author-intentionalist' position in hermeneutical theory.

From this position Luther dissented. His arguments against the Catholic reliance on tradition had the effect of shifting the focus of exegesis from the issue of identifying authorial intention to that of grasping the text's meaning in a dialectic of textual part and whole. He argued that the tradition is itself to be judged by its fidelity to the Scripture. While the role of divine inspiration in correct interpretation was central for Luther, he also stressed the crucial part played by scholarly training (especially a knowledge of the biblical languages). The point was that an apparently inspired reading (e.g., of the famous passage which plagued him, Romans 1:17) needed to be confirmed, not by consulting the tradition, but by showing its harmony with the rest of Scripture.[8]

---

[7]We will have a great deal to say below on the appropriateness of speaking of 'hypotheses' in hermeneutics.

[8]For Luther's own discussion of this method as used in his solution to the problem of Romans 1:17, one should read his *Preface* (1545) to the complete edition of his Latin works. The flavor of his exegetical practice can be tasted as well in the "selected Biblical prefaces," which—together with the *Preface* of 1545—are reprinted in English translation in Luther, 1961. A more detailed guide to his hermeneutical remarks (which are scattered all over his voluminous writings) can be found in G. Ebeling, 1942, 1969.

The hermeneutical consequence is this: against the Catholic reliance on tradition as a bridge back to the original understanding, Luther contends that Scripture is to be understood from itself alone (with, of course, the aid of inspiration). From our contemporary perspective we might paraphrase: the criterion of a correct interpretation is not the author's original intention *as something past*, but rather the intention embodied *in the text*. On Luther's view the meaning of the scriptural text is not something which stands *outside* of the text and which must be supplied to readers from an external source such as tradition. On the contrary: a studious reader equipped with a knowledge of the ancient languages and inspired by the gift of faith can discover the meaning within the text itself. Of course, not every passage is clear, but even the difficult sections can be understood in *the light of the Scripture as a whole*: the Scripture is *sui ipsius interpres*.

Here Luther has given an early formulation of the notion of the 'hermeneutical circle', the idea that the understanding of any part of a text and the understanding of the whole mutually condition each other. For him the circle is self-sufficient, and not (as it later was for Schleiermacher) an aid in the search for the author-intention. The correctness of an interpretation is to be measured by the immanent 'text-intention', the criterion of the harmony of parts and whole. Nonetheless Luther retains one central element of the traditional view, to wit the claim that it makes sense to speak of *the* one correct interpretation of the text—the one inspired by the Holy Spirit, as confirmed by its harmony with Scripture as a whole—versus many incorrect interpretations.

Gadamer's thesis of the 'openness of the text', i.e., of the *un*decidability of interpretation, has of course its own prehistory, in part within the Lutheran tradition. Gadamer's attitude toward Luther is ambivalent. On the one hand he treats Luther's approach to hermeneutics as the source of the (ultimately misleading) notion of the text's own unique intention; on the other hand (and more positively), he takes Luther to claim that a text is understood only in its *applicatio* by the reader to him/herself. This is to say, every correct new application or interpretation gives the text a new valid meaning, without thereby invalidating the former ones; as Gadamer puts it, "One understands *differently if one understands at all.*"[9]

From the point of view of the contemporary discussion we can say that many of the elements present in the Reformation dispute about correct exegesis continue to play important roles in philosophical hermeneutics. The author-intentionalism favored by the Catholic party retains its appeal far beyond the realm of Scripture scholarship, but the old problem of how we are nondogmatically to ascertain the author's intention remains acute. Luther's alternative was radical: no human mediator is necessary at all, for the text's meaning lies *in the text itself*, available to all who make use of the proper exegetical methods. However, this text-intentionalism has proven no more capable than its predecessor of providing a tribunal capable of settling, once and for all, interpretive disputes. The interpretation of a text, particularly of what Gadamer calls an 'eminent' text (whether scriptural, historical, literary, etc.), seems *de facto* a never-ending task. Accounting for this interminability seems to call, as we shall see below, for a quite different concept of text-meaning, the rudiments of which are present in Luther's notion of *applicatio*.

1.2 Nineteenth-Century Hermeneutical Theory

The dispute over scriptural exegesis constitutes prehistory for the contemporary German debate. According to Gadamer, in that prehistory hermeneutics was simply a tool used in disciplines concerned with the understanding of texts: an 'art' (or skill) of the Scripture scholar, jurist, and philologist. Not until the nineteenth century did this art—in Romanticism, the Historical School, and Dilthey—become progressively universalized so as to be thought of as the methodological principle which distinguishes the humanities. This develop-

[9]Gadamer, 1960/1975, p. 280/264. For Gadamer's positive debt to Luther see in particular Gadamer, 1972/1982.

ment provides the foil against which Gadamer unfolds his own thesis of the openness of the text.

Both Luther and his Catholic opponents were concerned exclusively with the practice of biblical interpretation. They were not interested in hermeneutics as a general epistemological, much less ontological, issue. Where they had regarded hermeneutics as a tool, a topic for manuals of rules designed to help the reader understand difficult passages, something new appears in the writings of Friedrich Schleiermacher: a deliberate attempt to display this tool in its 'dignified scientific form' by demonstrating that the 'special' hermeneutics of biblical and literary interpretation are mere species of a 'higher theory'. *Every* listener makes use of this theory, not only in coming to an understanding of all manner of texts ("überall, wo es Schriftsteller gibt,") but also

> *wherever* there is anything unfamiliar to [him] in the expression of thoughts through speech, although of course only to the extent that there is already something in common between him and the speaker.[10]

Schleiermacher's claim in this passage has two parts: first, that the art of interpretation is not reserved for particular, rather esoteric applications, e.g., to ancient literature, but is instead necessary for understanding *all uses of language*, written or spoken; and secondly, that all particular hermeneutical disciplines are branches of one and the same underlying theory. Since this theory is concerned with understanding *the linguistic expression of thoughts*, it has in all its forms, according to Schleiermacher, two aspects, grammatical and psychological (145). The former is of course concerned with the words of the text, the latter with the author's intention. Both aspects are essential to fulfilling the "task of hermeneutics . . .

---

[10]Friedrich Schleiermacher, 1959/1977, pp. 135–36/180–81, emphasis added. In the case of Schleiermacher we cite the German text reprinted in Gadamer, 1976a, and give our own English translation, though we also provide page numbers to the published translation.

[i.e,] to reconstruct (*nachbilden*) to the utmost the inner course of the compositional activity of the writer" (142/188).

The task of reconstruction, with its grammatical and psychological parts, follows the "hermeneutical principle, that, as the whole is of course understood from the individual, so too the individual can only be understood from the whole" (149/195–96).[11] As a result the labor of the interpreter proceeds "provisionally" from part to part, with each new part contributing to the understanding of what went before,

> until only at the end all the individual parts suddenly receive their full light and present themselves in pure and definite contours. (151–52/198)

Although Schleiermacher is concerned to emphasize the rational character of hermeneutics,[12] he nonetheless protests against F. A. Wolf's characterization of hermeneutics as "the art of discovering the thoughts of a writer from his text with insight that is absolutely necessary (*mit notwendiger Einsicht*)" (138/183).[13] Schleiermacher understands Wolf's characterization as requiring that the interpretation given be the only possible one in the light of the evidence. He finds the requirement too strong, for in many cases the evidence is simply not enough to rule out all other possibilities, and "as long as even one such possibility is not completely rejected, there can be no talk of necessity" (139/184). To be sure, a

---

[11]Schleiermacher credits Friedrich Ast, whose *Grundlinien der Grammatik, Hermeneutik und Kritik* was published in 1808, for making clear the central importance of this principle. Inspired by German Idealism, Ast phrased the principle in highly universal terms, for example: "The individual presupposes the idea of the whole, i.e., Spirit, which develops itself through the entire succession of individualities to perceptible life and finally returns into itself. With this flowing back of the Spirit into its original being the circle of explanation is closed . . . " F. Ast, 1808, sect. 82, reprinted in Gadamer, 1976a, our translation.

[12]According to Gadamer, Schleiermacher wishes to "safeguard the interpretation of the Bible from the claims of the theology of inspiration." Gadamer, 1976a, p. 31.

[13]Wolf, 1807, p. 37.

well-versed and insightful interpreter can reach something approaching utter certainty about the meaning of the text, but

> it is a completely different sort of certainty [from that which proof provides], indeed . . . [it is] more like divination, arising from the fact that the interpreter imagines himself as far as possible into the whole frame of mind of the writer. (139/185)

Schleiermacher, in the spirit of Romanticism, lays strong emphasis on the individual creative talent, the element of genius in the author. Hence he believes that the text is the "product of [the author's] personal idiosyncrasy" (140/185), and thus only an interpreter who is intimately in harmony with the author can hope to understand the work completely. This conception of hermeneutics, with its stress on "empathic understanding" and the need for a "kindred relationship of author and interpreter," plainly moves interpretation toward the general vicinity of the fine arts rather than the traditional sciences: reproduction of the original production.[14] It is certainly true that Schleiermacher stresses the role of a kind of interpretive artistry and the need for a special affinity between interpreter and author; and it is also true that he rejects Wolf's claim that hermeneutics can uncover the text's meaning "with insight that is absolutely necessary." Nonetheless, he does not mean thereby to deny that interpretation can be

---

[14]Cf. Gadamer, 1960/1975, pp. 175/164 ff. It is this conception which has been attacked by the Vienna Circle and English-speaking Neopositivists. Their attitude was that if there is to be anything objective or scientific about interpretive disciplines, then these disciplines must use methods which are teachable and procedures which are intersubjective and repeatable. See T. Abel, 1953. Schleiermacher's 'empathic understanding' could be no more than the sort of inspiration which is common to all sciences *in the context of discovery* (Neurath is said to have likened it to a good cup of coffee, which gives the researcher this or that new impulse); the scientific part of interpretation, however, must consist in testing by objective methods the interpretive hypotheses which inspirations (of whatever sort) have suggested.

certain, nor that hermeneutics can be, in some sense, scientific, but it remains vague just what that sense is.

Clarifying this very question was part of the task which Wilhelm Dilthey set himself. One of his central theses represents an important and potentially fruitful challenge to empiricist assumptions. Dilthey, no less than Hume, regards private experience (*Erlebnisse*) as the basis of our knowledge of the world. But Hume conceived the relationship among the items of experience (impressions and ideas) in an essentially atomistic fashion, i.e., either they *naturally* give rise one to another according to "principles of association" (the principles being resemblance, contiguity in time or place, and cause and effect), or they are combined "in the fancy" for what Hume calls "philosophical" comparison.[15] Nowhere in the *Treatise* is there talk of part-whole or meaning-relations among the ideas and impressions.

Dilthey, on the other hand, speaks of the "inner connection" among experiences, each of which is "referred to a self, whose part it is; it is structurally connected with other parts to form a context. In everything pertaining to mind [or spirit, i.e., *Geist*] we find connectedness . . . "[16] The mark of such 'contexts' is that the parts are meaningful: they determine the meaning of the whole, while at the same time their own meaning is determined by that of the whole.[17] So too on the level of self-awareness, we do not regard ourselves as bundles of atomic impressions, rather one sees oneself as the central character in an ongoing story, in which the various parts bear meaningful relationships to each other. The art form corre-

---

[15]David Hume, 1739–40, Book I, part I, sections 4 and 5. A very recent version of Hume's project is to be found in J. Fodor, 1987.

[16]Dilthey, 1927/1976, p. 195/211.

[17]We shall suggest—in section 3, below—that it is precisely in the distinction between meaning-connections and empirical connections that the difference between interpretations and scientific hypotheses lies.

sponding to this basic level of self-understanding is the autobiography.[18]

The Neo-Kantian task which Dilthey set himself was to show how, from the narrow basis of one's own private experiences, each of us builds up an intersubjective framework consisting of persons, the various expressions of their experiences, the institutions of the social world, and so on. He hoped to show that "the categories of the world of mind and spirit"—to wit: life, experience, expression, understanding, meaning, will, purpose, etc.—have "objective value." Just as did his phenomenalistic counterparts in the empiricist tradition, Dilthey argued that the transition from private to intersubjective is accomplished by inferences of analogy and induction. 'Analogy' leads us from a familiar expression we encounter in another person (a gesture, an action, a speech-act) to a supposition about the inner experience which is thereby expressed. 'Induction' is more inclusive; by it we infer the character (or 'inner context') of another on the basis of a variety of his or her life-expressions. Both kinds of inferences are probabilistic in nature. Dilthey concludes that "the process of understanding is itself to be conceived as induction" (220/231).

The natural sciences are also built on induction, for example inferring an underlying law from a series of cases. However, in the "sciences of the world of mind and spirit" (*Geisteswissenschaften*) the induction leads to what Dilthey

---

[18]One interesting aspect of Dilthey's approach, which however we can do no more than mention here, is the suggestion it offers toward a solution to the Humean problem of personal identity. Where Hume found only atomistic relations among the constituents of his inner world (hence finding the soul to be like nothing so much as "a republic or commonwealth"), Dilthey sees meaningfulness as an essential element of such constituents. Hence for him each has an implicit internal relation to a whole. He might liken the soul to a story, which requires both a narrator and an inner connectedness of the parts. This 'hermeneutical' conception of the self has been discussed by, among others, A. MacIntyre, 1981, chap. 15.

calls "a structure, a system of order which gathers together the cases *as parts of a whole*" (220/231, emphasis added). He draws from this sort of fact the lesson that, since the categories (basically having to do with the concept of meaning) which guide such conceptualization are "alien to the knowledge of nature as such" (196–97/212), it is natural that the *Geisteswissenschaften*—i.e., the 'humanities' and (some of) the social sciences—differ in kind and method from the sciences of nature. Their method consists not of experimentation, but of understanding and interpreting. These age-old skills (*Techniken*) are the basis of philology, history, scriptural exegesis, and the like, "and the *science* of [these skills] is hermeneutics" (217/228, emphasis added).

It is fair to say that the major German hermeneutical theorists of the nineteenth century agreed that the hermeneutical disciplines are 'separate but equal', i.e., scientific yet different in kind from the natural sciences. The interpretive goal, Schleiermacher had held, is to bring to light something hidden, hidden not so much in the text as in the psyche of the writer. This is one kind of what we might call "objective interpretation," the *prima facie* attractive view that what an honest interpreter is after is the meaning which a text in fact *has*, quite independently of any interpreting which might be done. But a 'hermeneutical objectivist' need not think of the *author's* intention as the criterion of the correct interpretation. He or she may also, following Luther, contend (as did Monroe Beardsley and the New Critics) that something like the 'text-intention' is what the interpreter is after.[19] Alternatively one may think that the correct interpretation is the one which captures the understanding which the text's original audience had. All three views agree that the meaning of the text is an objective fact, something which in principle could be discovered once and for all. Thus interpretation is, epistemologically

---

[19]Beardsley is one of the most prominent contemporary foes of Schleiermachean (or author-oriented) hermeneutics. See Beardsley, 1970.

speaking, the process of verifying, falsifying, confirming, etc., various *meaning-hypotheses*.

From the point of view of the contemporary debate we can conclude that the bulk of what Dilthey says puts him squarely in the same objectivist tradition as Schleiermacher and the Reformation parties. But the Neo-Kantian, constructivistic nature of his project raises at least a faint doubt that on his view the meaning of the text is unambiguously 'out there'. In a postscript to the essay from which we have been quoting, Dilthey, as he does so often, draws a contrast between the understanding of a text and "the knowledge of nature." Here, however, even the latter contains a (no doubt transcendentally conceived) element of subjectivity:

> In the knowledge of nature we take as our basis the image as solid quantity given in intuition. The object, as the permanent which makes the alteration of the images explicable, is *constructed out of the images*. (227, emphasis added)

It would seem to follow from Dilthey's view that in the hermeneutical disciplines there will be a 'constructing' analogous to that in the cognition of nature. But over and above this subjective contribution of the mind, hermeneutics confronts 'objects' quite different from those of nature. The words of a text, for example, are precisely *not* a "solid quantity given in intuition." Dilthey calls them "something determined-undetermined," meaning presumably that their significance depends in part on that of the whole to which they belong. But since the meaning of that whole is itself determined by the meaning of the parts, interpretation is "an attempt to determine, an *interminable process* [*ein Niezuendekommen*—literally 'a never coming to an end'], a shift between part and whole" (p. 227, emphasis added).

Now if the process of interpretation is interminable and if its 'object' (a meaningful text or other 'life-expression') is 'constructed' in the hermeneutical process, in what sense can we speak of interpretation as 'objective'? Here, as with Luther, we find the hint that the practice of the interpretation of texts reveals what we could call the 'constructivistic' nature of text-meaning. Dilthey did not phrase the issue of the status of hermeneutics in this form, but the question has come to be of central importance in twentieth-century German philosophy.

The hermeneutic development in the nineteenth century is, on the whole, an expansion on the Reformation dispute: it both confirms and universalizes the earlier positions, while maintaining the general agreement that interpretation is finite and objective. Interpretation aims at (and, in favorable cases, attains) the one truth—the one sense of the text—which is objective in that it is 'there', either in the text or in the author. But with the notion of the "interminability of the hermeneutical circle," mentioned in passing by Dilthey and reminiscent of Luther's concept of *applicatio*, another conception of interpretation seems to announce its arrival on the scene.

1.3 Constructivism

We have noted that the hermeneutical tradition up to and including Dilthey was dominated by what we may call a straightforward, 'naive realism' (or 'objectivism') about the meaning of texts: texts *have*, virtually by definition, a unique meaning, one that is in principle *determinable* by the reader (though as we have seen there was disagreement over the questions of what the meaning consists in and how the interpreter is to determine it). To this extent interpretations were regarded on all sides as *decidable*. A contemporary version of objectivism is represented in this volume by Stegmüller, while the essays of Gadamer and Specht present views that are in important respects non-objectivist or, as we shall style them, 'constructivist'. The experience is familiar to all interpreters that the process of interpreting the text *de facto* goes on and on.[20] For constructivists this fact assumes a completely

---

[20]So that, for example, there seems no end to the new readings given to a play such as *Hamlet* or to passages in the Scripture. Cf., for the former, M. Weitz, 1964; for the latter compare K. Stendahl's article, "Biblical Theology," in Buttrick et al., 1962; Stendahl's translational analogy is reminiscent of Gadamer's approach to the interpretation of

new significance. It is no longer taken as indicating that the true interpretation has simply *not yet been found*, but rather that there is *no such finally correct interpretation*.[21] This insight stems from the conception that the text is not an 'object out there' independent of its interpretations and capable of serving as an arbiter of their correctness. The *interpretandum* is not simply *there*, its true nature waiting to be discovered: it must be constructed in the process of reading.

As a hermeneutical objectivist, Stegmüller in spite of his rejection of the autonomy thesis, is substantially a part of the hermeneutical tradition sketched above. With their respective versions of constructivism, however, Gadamer and Specht represent a substantial twentieth-century departure from that tradition (though, as we saw, there are constructivist hints in the thinking of Luther and Dilthey). The inspiration for this departure was derived from the thought of Heidegger (in the case of Gadamer), and from that of Wittgenstein (for Specht). We now turn to a brief description of those sources.

1.3.a Heidegger. The main historical source which Gadamer taps for his criticism of the very notion that a text has a uniquely correct interpretation is Martin Heidegger's *Sein und Zeit*, with its claim that understanding is made possible by the prejudices of the interpreter's time or epoch which disclose and constitute being (and, therefore, the text). Thus every epoch has its own valid understanding of an 'eminent' text. Gadamer's thesis of the openness of the text rests

---

Rilke's *Elegies* in essay 2, below. None of this is to deny that the interpretation of some texts has *de facto* come to an end; this occurs, however, not because *the* correct reading has been discovered, but rather because the text is no longer considered of interest. One example of this loss of interest is the neglect into which the Metaphysical Poets (Donne, Marvell, Crashaw, et al.) fell for some two hundred years (until Grierson and Eliot rehabilitated them).

[21]We stress that here (and in our Conclusion) we are speaking of philosophical and methodological reflection on the practice of interpretation, not of the interpreter's own conception of his or her task.

on the notion that *all* understanding proceeds from 'positive prejudices' (or 'pre-judgments') of the reader. Thus the circle of understanding is no longer to be regarded as a characteristic of hermeneutic method, but rather as a fundamental, ontological aspect of human being. Gadamer explicitly credits Heidegger with these insights.

According to Heidegger, we are not simply entities or 'objects in the world', rather we find ourselves 'hurled' into a network of institutions, purposes, plans, tools, implements, et al., toward all of which our basic stance is 'understanding' (in a very broad sense). Heidegger contends that at this level things such as chairs or trees are not regarded as 'physical objects', but rather as implements in, or constituents of, the plans, purposes, etc., of our lives. Understanding something as a chair in this spontaneous, everyday sense (which is characterized by 'prudence' or 'concern' with our needs) involves what Heidegger calls our 'fore-having'.[22] Understanding, as a basic attitude of human existence, can of course be made self-conscious and 'cultivated' as interpretation. To interpret something which we 'fore-have' presupposes the selection of an aspect, a target or *telos* at which we (consciously or otherwise) aim.[23] This aiming involves concepts or a point of view, what Heidegger calls 'fore-sight' ('*Vorsicht*', literally 'caution'). Finally, the interpretation itself is formulated in the concepts we make use of to characterize the *interpretandum*, and will be in the first instance what seem most 'natural' to the interpreter; it is grounded, Heidegger says, in his or her 'fore-conception' (*Vorgriff*, literally 'anticipation', but etymologically 'fore-grasp'). As a result,

---

[22]In German *Vorhabe*, a Heideggerian coinage akin to *Vorhaben*, 'plan', 'intention', 'purpose'; the coinage suggests that understanding the chair is a matter of fitting it into an (already prepared) place in the aforementioned network of goals and the like.

[23]Compare Gadamer's opening remarks in essay 2 below: "All interpretation is one-sided. It aims at a target, an aspect which can lay no claim to uniqueness."

> Interpretation is never a presuppositionless grasp of something given . . . [For] that which at first 'is there' [in a text] is nothing but the natural, undiscussed fore-opinion of the interpreter, which in every attempt at interpretation is necessarily present as that which is from the start 'posited' with any interpretation at all, i.e., is pre-given in fore-having, fore-sight, and fore-conception.[24]

For Heidegger the task of scholarly interpretation is that of

> not accepting from flashes of inspiration and popular notions a pretence of its own fore-having, fore-sight, and fore-conception, but rather to work these out of the subject matter itself and thereby to secure the topic under study.[25]

All understanding, scholarly or otherwise, thus manifests a 'circle-structure' which is rooted in our nature as beings whose stance toward the world is marked by (pre-)understanding. As such we always and necessarily project our own largely subconscious, teleologically structured conceptual net on everything we encounter, only gradually becoming aware that this or that putative feature of the 'object' is really part of our own 'fore-conception'. Heidegger is not thinking in individual terms here, but means rather that the concepts which one unreflectively projects are those of one's 'time' (or epoch or culture). It is *only* in the framework of such projection that one understands the 'objects' (including texts) of other epochs. At the same time it is only in this latter act of understanding, directed now at 'the Other', that one becomes aware at all of one's own fore-having, fore-sight, and fore-conception. Since all interpreting of the Other must begin by 'constructing' the text from the standpoint of the interpreter, there is simply no question of finding *the* uniquely and finally correct interpretation.

---

[24]Heidegger, 1927/1962, sect. 32, p. 150/191–92.

[25]Heidegger, 1927/1962, p. 153/195, cited below by Gadamer, in the first essay, pp. 70–71. Cf. also Gadamer's second essay, p. 81.

Heidegger's own major hermeneutical labor is directed at the history of Western metaphysics, in which he finds a one-sided attachment to the subject-object distinction. The very conception of an 'entity' about which we 'make objective assertions' is, he argues, an abstraction from the "original act of interpretation," which "lies not in a theoretical assertion, but rather in a prudential/attentive" use of the things we encounter in our world (1927/1962, p. 157/200).[26] In other words, Western philosophy has succumbed to the temptation to portray our *use* of language solely as consisting of propositions which purport to picture or reflect 'facts' or 'objects'. A more elaborate critique along these lines was developed by Wittgenstein.

1.3.b Wittgenstein. According to Specht (in essay 4) one of the characteristic features of literary-critical practice is that an author's own interpretation of his/her work, as well as accurate author-intentional interpretations by others, are very often rejected by other critics on the grounds that they fail to capture the meaning *of the text*. But then 'meaning of the text' must signify something quite different from 'the author's intention'. On Specht's analysis of this situation, at least one common and important kind of interpretation essentially involves a construal, indeed what he calls a 'construction', of the text by the reader; hence no such interpretation can lay claim to a final correctness guaranteed by 'theory-neutral' facts. Thus 'meaning' here amounts to 'what has been construed by the reader'. This holds for psychoanalysis no less than for literary criticism, for there are no psychoanalytically uninterpreted facts to confirm the analyst's interpretation. But such construal is neither subjective nor arbitrary. Specht points in both cases to existing canons or criteria for the evaluation of interpretations.[27]

---

[26]As noted above, Gadamer sees an exception to what Heidegger criticizes here in Luther's 'existential' conception of the hermeneutical circle.

[27]For a detailed presentation of the case of psychoanalytic dream interpretation see especially Specht, 1981.

To the extent that, in respect to decidability, practice differs in the hermeneutical disciplines from what it is in the natural sciences, Specht seems to support a form of the autonomy thesis.

Specht's claim that there are undecidable interpretations in literary criticism and psychoanalysis can be understood against the backdrop of a constructivist line of argument in the later philosophy of Wittgenstein. In the *Blue Book* Wittgenstein raises the question, "What's an explanation of meaning?" and he says that if we begin by posing *this* question, we free ourselves from the temptation to answer the question, "What is the meaning of *x*?" always in one and the same way:

> The questions "What is length?" "What is meaning?" "What is the number one?" etc., produce in us a mental cramp. We feel that we can't point to anything in reply to them and yet ought to point to something.[28]

The point of an explanation of meaning, Wittgenstein contends, is to clarify the use of an expression; hence it sometimes *can*, but *need not*, be given by an ostensive definition (in the case of words) or by citing truth-conditions (in the case of sentences). To give favored rank to ostension or to truth-conditions in the theory of meaning is to succumb to a form of semantic realism. Realism presupposes that the differentiations which we draw in language are the attempt to depict the differentiations which are already there in reality. For this reason, when we define a word or give the meaning of a sentence, what we do is to indicate the object or state of affairs meant. The definitions we give (e.g., of the words 'gold', 'acid', 'the number one', etc.) are accordingly correct or incorrect, and reality (rather than the language-community) decides the matter. Someone who thinks this way succumbs to the temptation to imagine that many (all?) of the correct concepts (i.e., those which the ideal science would ultimately discover and use) *are* already defined by reality, and have

---

[28]L. Wittgenstein, 1958, p. 1.

either been discovered already or else are waiting to be. In this sense a realist might claim that (apparently) we *have found* the correct definition of a particular biological species (say, swans) through the scientific discovery and decoding of its DNA. Thus the realist introduces a particular notion of 'correct definition', namely one which defines the concepts which actually apply, whether we know it or not, to the phenomena in question.[29]

According to Wittgenstein, however, the temptation to realism ought to be resisted. The definition of concepts is something which *we do*, and thus they *are not* defined until *we* define them. Consider the discovery of Cook's black swans: it is not predetermined whether these birds are 'really swans'. All we can say is that, if we decide to treat them as such, then we reject whiteness as a defining characteristic of swanhood (choosing instead some other characteristic, such as a certain morphology or a specific kind of DNA). If, on the other hand, we decide not to treat them as swans, then by this very decision we take whiteness to be *ceteris paribus* a criterial attribute which distinguishes swans from other birds, including Cook's 'black swans'. "All swans are white" will be a false empirical proposition in the first case, and a definition in the second. The difference lies in the use we make of the proposition, and this use is determined by an arbitrary convention.[30]

Constructivism in this sense asserts that the meaning of a linguistic expression is not something given before we have constructed it. There is therefore no definition before the construction has been done. Prior to our deciding what use we will make of "All swans are white," it is simply not fixed whether Cook's black birds are swans or not. The description

---

[29]We shall look more closely at one variety of realism (Putnam's) below.

[30]"Consider: 'The only correlate in language to a natural necessity is an arbitrary rule. That is the only thing which one can draw off from this natural necessity into a proposition.'" Wittgenstein, 1953, §372, our translation.

of linguistic usage shows which decisions have been made, and thus 'what we mean' (in the constructivist sense).

Of course no contemporary scientist would treat "All swans are white" as (part of) the definition of swanhood. But what about a specific genetic code? Is not a definition of the form "All and only swans have the genetic code x,y,z" a deep insight into the nature of swans? *Could* we then *not* find a swan with a different genetic code? If a scientist claims that this is simply not possible, the philosophical question is, on what is the scientist insisting? Here the realist would say that the scientist is insisting on a particularly deep empirical feature of swans. But to say that no exceptions can be admitted to "All and only swans have the genetic code x,y,z" *is* precisely to use that assertion as a convention, one which regulates the linguistic use of 'swan'.[31] Wittgenstein says that the modes of behavior which find expression in such 'deep' conventions constitute 'forms of life'. To reject, therefore, the proposition that black swans are true swans is to reject the language-game that is modern biology (with unforeseeable consequences for the remainder of those of our forms of life—e.g., medicine, biotechnology, etc.—which are *interwoven* with this language-game).[32]

What is meant by calling Wittgenstein's approach 'constructivistic' is this: the essential, that whose contrary seems

---

[31]W. V. O. Quine has developed similar arguments, e.g., in Quine, 1953 and 1960. Like Wittgenstein, Quine believes that holding fast to particular sentences, "come what may," is not determined by experience, and is in this sense arbitrary. Unlike Wittgenstein, he does not think that these sentences which are immunized by convention from empirical rejection represent *linguistic* conventions governing our use of language. For Wittgenstein's view see, for example, his 1953, §251: "Of course, here 'I can't imagine the opposite' doesn't mean: my powers of imagination are unequal to the task. These words are a defence against something whose form makes it look like an empirical proposition, but which is really a grammatical one . . . Example: 'Every rod has a length.' That means something like: we *call* something (or *this*) 'the length of a rod'—but nothing 'the length of a sphere'" (emphasis added).

[32]Cf. Wittgenstein, 1953, §241.

unimaginable, is not found in reality, it is rather "expressed by grammar."[33] And since it is expressed by grammar, it follows arbitrary rules, is construed according to conventions. What a conceptual investigation reveals as part of the grammar of the language-game *is* just what earlier philosophy thought of as essence.

Let us now ask what it means, in conjunction with this constructivist view of meaning, to speak of *interpretations* as undecidable. Take, for example, any pretwentieth-century interpretation of *Hamlet*; it is likely to include the view that Hamlet intends to avenge his father's murder. For many generations this proposition seemed self-evident to literary critics, since Hamlet himself says as much in the play. But the question does arise, why then does he *not* kill Claudius? One kind of answer traditionally given is that he has the character of a procrastinator. Early in this century, however, and in the wake of Freud's investigations, Otto Rank (1915) and others argued that Hamlet does not really intend to avenge the murder, for what in fact preoccupies him is the question of his mother's sinful union with Claudius. A 'semantical realist' (who is almost certain to be what we above called a 'hermeneutical objectivist') thinks that it is a necessary truth that *either* Hamlet intends to avenge the murder *or* that he does not (i.e., that the traditional view and the view of Rank are incompatible and that one of them must be true), and thus regards the question as a decidable one on the basis of the facts (author's intention, text-intention, or whatever).

However, an alternative Wittgensteinian approach of the kind espoused in this volume by Specht contends that the realist overlooks the element of construction in literary interpretation, i.e., the *construal* of the text by the reader. The traditional interpreter takes Hamlet's expression of what he intends at face value, and must accordingly explain away the young prince's inaction, for example, in terms of his indecisive character. Rank, however, from his psychoanalytic per-

---

[33]Wittgenstein, 1953, §371.

spective, takes the inaction as central, and—on the basis of the notion of the Oedipus complex—sees Hamlet's expression of what he intends as sincere but self-deceptive. The philosophical point is that the literary-critical question whether or not Hamlet wants to avenge the murder is not decidable *independently* of a global reading (construal) of the text, and such readings are to a certain extent arbitrary. If one abandons one interpretation in favor of another, this may seem to be the result of a new intuition into the 'real essence' of the text; but it would be more correct to say instead that such a change represents the decision to construe the text in the new way.[34] Such a decision might be a rejection of the *kind* of interpretation that Rank gives, i.e., of the language-game of psychoanalytic literary criticism; or it might be merely a rejection of Rank's specific reading.[35]

1.4. Summation

The contemporary discussion in German philosophical hermeneutics has been devoted in large part to issues concerned with the decidability of textual interpretation. Up to this point we have tried to show how that discussion arose out of earlier controversies, first over scriptural exegesis, and then over the scientific status of the humanities. If we characterize as 'hermeneutical objectivism' the view that for all (or most) literary texts there is in principle a uniquely correct interpretation, then we can say that Anglo-American reflection on interpretation has, until the past decade, been dominated by the dispute between various kinds of hermeneutical objectivism or realism. But the twentieth-century German scene has been one in which non-objectivist views abound; and our survey,

---

[34]Compare with this Wittgenstein's remark about following the rule '+ 2', in his 1953, §186.

[35]Note that the point made here applies regardless of whether Rank and other psychoanalytic critics themselves adopt a realist metacritical position and regard their own interpretations as decidably true or false. From a Wittgensteinian perspective they would then be just as confused as any other hermeneutical objectivists (realists).

here and in section 2, shows that recently (and increasingly) those views have drawn on the work of philosophers (especially Wittgenstein) whose writings are in the mainstream of Anglo-American philosophy. Our historical overview suggests that we can distinguish two major points of view in philosophical hermeneutics, using as our criterion of distinction the differing attitudes toward the question of the decidability of interpretations:

The first, representing the nearly unanimous opinion of pretwentieth-century hermeneutical theory, says that *interpretations are decidable*, and they are so either by virtue of the author's intention, or by virtue of the text-intention. However, the fact that on this view there is a uniquely correct interpretation corresponding to the unique meaning of the text does not rule out the possibility of an undecid*edness* that, in at least one version (as we shall see below, when we discuss Putnam), approaches undecidability. According to objectivism one can nonetheless specify what the truth of the interpetation would consist in. This is the formal sense of saying that an omniscient being would be in a position to decide on the interpretation's truth-value.

The second point of view says, on constructivist grounds, that *interpretations are not decidable*; here there are two similar, though distinct, positions:

i. Texts exist only in being-read, and every interpretation gives the text a new reading within a framework constituted by the pre-judgments of the reader's time, epoch, or culture; thus there is no such thing as 'the one text' capable of serving as the touchstone for the correctness of interpretations from different epochs. This position entails undecidability in principle.

ii. To think of the 'true meaning' of the text as something finished and completed, ready to be *discovered*, is a 'philosophical confusion.' It stems from the fact that we tend to misunderstand those interpretations which we consider irrefutably obvious as straightforwardly empirical claims expressing essential features of the text itself. But in fact such interpretations presuppose an arbitrary, generally tacit *construal* of the text. This position also entails undecidability in principle.

We proceed now to a detailed discussion of the four essays translated in this volume.

2. Overview of the Essays

To reflect the chronological development of the recent German hermeneutics debate, we begin (here, as in the ordering of the translations themselves) with Gadamer's "On the Circle of Understanding" (published in 1959), following this with an application of his ideas on hermeneutics in his literary critical essay, "Mythopoetic Inversion in Rilke's *Duino Elegies*" (composed in 1966). Both essays, in which Gadamer develops further a number of Heidegger's contributions to philosophical hermeneutics, represent major aspects of the tradition with which Stegmüller finds fault in essay 3 (1979). One of the latter's central tenets is in turn criticized by Specht in essay 4 (1984).

2.1 Gadamer's Philosophical Hermeneutics

Gadamer's central thesis is that in the hermeneutical disciplines a particular epistemological ideal is out of place, the ideal of the determinate 'object' (here: the text) about which successive generations of scholars attain progressively deeper knowledge. This ideal—a form of what we have been calling 'decidability'—is said to overlook an 'ontological feature' of understanding, namely its 'prejudice-structure'; for there are not only the negative prejudices which the epistemological tradition has regarded as hindrances to deeper knowledge, but also 'positive pre-judgments' which make all understanding possible. In the humanities, in particular, the prejudice- (or circle-) structure of understanding makes it possible in the first place for us even to begin to comprehend a text, while the conscious confrontation with the text's 'horizon' requires that we confront those of our prejudices which hinder genuine understanding; thus the process is one which requires, and makes possible, a kind of self-knowledge.[36]

The essay "On the Circle of Understanding" offers the most concise statement of Gadamer's mature thought.[37] In it Gadamer begins his discussion of the hermeneutical circle with a historical overview of the notion. A portion of that history we discussed in section 1 above. On his view the circle was regarded—prior to Heidegger—largely as a method, an interpretive movement which runs "back and forth in the text and [is] consummated when the text itself [is] completely understood" (p. 68). To this formalistic account of the circle as a method applied by the interpreter Heidegger opposed an "ontological" account: so far from being a tool which one might apply or not, the circle of understanding expresses the deep fact of the "prejudice-structure" of human understanding itself. We are able to understand, say, an ancient text just to the extent that we have 'pre-judgments' about the subject matter of the text. At the same time Heidegger claims that the task of the interpreter is to resist deceptive "flashes of inspiration and popular notions" so as to let the text itself speak through us.

There is an air of paradox to this Heideggerian thesis, as if the interpreter's pre-judgments or 'prejudices' are both an indispensable ally and an implacable foe: although our effort is directed to seeing with the eyes of the text, the very prejudices which enable us to make the attempt ensure that our success will always remain partial, that the eyes through

---

[36]For Gadamer the central notion of the 'hermeneutical situation' (or perspective) of the reader goes together with that of the 'horizon of prejudices' (or pre-judgments) which bounds any such perspective. But the text too has its own horizon, and the process of understanding is, as we shall see below, a matter of 'fusing' the two horizons.

[37]Composed for the Heidegger *Festschrift* in 1959—just as Gadamer's masterwork, *Wahrheit und Methode*, was going to press—"On the Circle" contains important passages which were taken over word for word into the crucial central section of the *magnum opus*.

which we look will always remain our own.[38] It is this thesis which Gadamer attempts to explicate in essay 1 and to apply in essay 2.

The notion of *translation*, so important in recent Anglo-American philosophy, provides us a key for understanding Gadamer.[39] If we think of the study of *texts*—classical, scriptural, historical, literary, philosophical, etc.—as the core of the humanities, then the notion of translation is obviously of central importance in humanistic disciplines. This is so not only for ancient or foreign-language texts, but also for literature and philosophy composed in one's own tongue. As Gadamer points out in essay 2 (p. 81), even the few decades separating the Rilke of the 1920s from the German-speaking reader of the 1960s sufficed to create the "distance of an immensely altered life-feeling." Indeed, literary works quite generally confront a reader with the task of bridging the chasm that separates his or her real-life world from the imaginary world—at once (more or less) similar to the reader's own world, and yet different too—in which the literary action unfolds. Thus contemporary poetry and fiction, no less than biblical exegesis, manifest what Gadamer calls (in "On the Circle") the "polarity of familiarity and strangeness on which the

---

[38]E. Rothacker expresses both aspects of this peculiar process of knowing: "Until suddenly, often after a lifetime, the scholar with a peculiar 'I've got it' believes he sees all the lines [of his/her research] without exception ordered in perspective and thereby understood. What he then saw in the vanishing point of those lines was all along face to face, a human eye. Here, where in something with an objective meaning a subjective significance flashes upon the scene, not isolated behind the objective, but rather illuminating it, the humanities see the goal of understanding." Rothacker, 1948, p. 126, our translation. Such knowledge is interpersonal communication, but the question remains, *Whose* eye does the scholar behold?

[39]Trained as a classical philologist himself, Gadamer gives an extended translational analogy at the start of "On the Circle," and the notion also figures prominently in his essay on Rilke.

task of hermeneutics is based" (p. 76), a polarity which both calls for translation and makes it possible.[40]

The difficulty for the interpreter is not so much how to rise above his or her own 'familiar' prejudices to an appreciation of the worldview represented in the text; it is rather, how the interpreter is even to *become aware* of his or her prejudices as such. Gadamer agrees with the Romantic hermeneuticists that understanding the text, as opposed to understanding what *we* have read into it, requires a separating out of our prejudices. This may sound like the familiar pious advice to bracket out one's own opinions,[41] but this cannot be what Gadamer intends, for he insists that

> far from it being the case that whoever listens to someone else or approaches a literary text must bring along no pre-opinion about the content and must forget all his own opinions, it is rather the case that openness for the opinion of the other or of the text will always include setting it in relation to the whole of one's own opinions . . . ("On the Circle," below, p. 72)

In other words, our prejudices cannot be simply bracketed, since it is in terms of them that we understand whatever and whenever we understand.

What Gadamer here fails to make clear, however, is the complexity of what he labels 'prejudices'. First of all, as he points out elsewhere, there are *two kinds* of 'pre-judgment' involved, 'formal' and 'material', the former concerning "the

---

[40]Gadamer is, of course, aware of the hermeneutical challenge of contemporary artistic productions, but he initially chose to put them in a category of their own because of the special challenge their contemporaneousness represents to "academic consciousness" (see "On the Circle," p. 76). More recently, however, Gadamer has revised this view: it is *distance*, not necessarily *temporal* distance, "which makes [the] hermeneutical task solvable." Gadamer, 1986, p. 304.

[41]In the mid-nineteenth century Ranke went so far as to speak of the 'self-extinction' of the interpreter. Cf. Gadamer's discussion of this point, in his 1960/1975, p. 198/186.

rules of grammar, the stylistic devices, and the art of composition, on all of which the text is based"; while the latter concern "the subject matter relation which obtains between the text's statement and our own understanding of the subject."[42] Understanding cannot begin until we recognize the kind of text we are dealing with and the subject matter it is about. The formal prejudices, as constitutive, are plainly positive, they enable us to understand. But we cannot simply say that the material prejudices are 'negative' in that they seduce us into attributing to the text our views (our 'horizon'), for that would be to overlook the role they play in establishing a commonality between us and the text.[43] Rilke's invocation of angels is a case in point: they are indeed superhuman beings (and hence are rightly called 'angels', i.e., our word 'angel' is rightly used of them), but we go astray if we think they are *the familiar angels of Judaeo-Christian theology* (see essay 2, pp. 81 ff.). Our material pre-judgments show us that the text is about something familiar (and are hence positive), our mistaken prejudice is to think that this something is completely familiar.

Under what conditions can our negative prejudices be 'separated out'? Gadamer's answer is that they can be separated out just when the normal and natural agreement between reader and text about the subject matter is disturbed. To see what he means, we need first to look at Gadamer's explication of his puzzling and deliberately ambiguous motto, "to understand means primarily to understand [oneself in] the subject matter" (*sich in der Sache verstehen*—"On the Circle," p. 75).[44]

---

[42]Gadamer, 1972/1982, p. 333/98.

[43]This tends to belie, incidentally, Stegmüller's assertion that the notion of a 'positive prejudice' flies in the face of ordinary usage and is given no explicit definition by the hermeneuticists (see below, essay 3, pp. 106 f).

[44]Three related conceptual elements are packed into the italicized phrase: a) *to know one's way about the subject-matter*, i.e., to have the

Let us begin by looking at what Gadamer regards as the 'primary', the 'normal and natural' situation of reading (e.g., reading a newspaper account or a letter from a friend), that is, where we simply accept as true what we read. The priority of factually agreeing with the Other as a condition of understanding him or her is likely to be familiar to the Anglo-American reader from Donald Davidson's reflections on translation. As part of his Tarskian truth-theoretic approach to semantics, Davidson has argued that translation of individual utterances is only possible against the backdrop of a translation *scheme* (or manual), and the formulation of any such scheme requires that we credit the Other a priori with believing a great deal of what we believe.[45] Gadamer, whose semantical views—we shall argue—are very different from Davidson's, nonetheless insists on a very similar notion, which he calls "the anticipation of perfection" ("On the Circle," pp. 74 ff.), i.e., the expectation of coherence and correctness in what we read. One result is that whatever we are able to read with comprehension will perforce have a certain amount of plausibility and familiarity for us, we will feel it "belongs" to us and we to it ("On the Circle," p. 75), a point that is reminiscent of Davidson's rejection of the notion of radically disparate conceptual schemes.[46]

Now, according to Gadamer, we as readers become aware

---

sort of general know-how and know-what of a person well-versed about such things; b) *to agree with the text*, i.e., to believe what it tells us; and c) *to understand oneself* (in the confrontation with the text's viewpoint). The German *sich verstehen* can, in the appropriate contexts, bear all three readings. Gadamer's idea seems to be that *sich verstehen* (*s.v.*) in sense a) is a general condition of *s.v.* in sense b) (we have to know something about the content in order to be able to agree or disagree); and where *s.v.* in sense b) proves impossible (i.e., where there is a break in our normal and natural acceptance, as readers, of what we are told), *s.v.* in sense c) is (or at least can be) the result. It is only a slight exaggeration to say that in this motto Gadamer's entire philosophical hermeneutics receives compressed expression.

[45]Cf., among many examples, Davidson, 1980, p. 221.

[46]See Davidson, 1984, essay 13.

of our 'inappropriate prejudices', the kind that distort the text, when our "anticipation of perfection" is frustrated. At various points we are unable either to understand or to agree with the text. *This* sort of encounter brings into the open the reader's own beliefs as such. It is here that understanding what the text says requires of the reader the suspension of the prejudice which has come to light. But, continues Gadamer,

> all suspension of judgments—consequently and above all the suspension of prejudices—has in logical terms the structure of a question. The essence of a question is to open up possibilities and keep them open. ("Circle," p. 77)

Thus the struggle to understand a text, even if carried out in the context of academic research, forces readers to confront *themselves*, i.e., their own subliminal opinions about the subject matter with which the text deals. For the past, and past ways of looking at things (including especially the text in question), live on *in our ingrained prejudices*: this is the "essential reality of history in understanding itself" ("On the Circle," p. 78), and Gadamer calls it 'the history of influence' (*Wirkungsgeschichte*). The hermeneutical awareness of this situation, the self-confrontation (and hence confrontation with the past) engendered by the attempt to understand the meaning of a text, is that to which Gadamer gives the intimidating label "consciousness of the history of influence" (*wirkungsgeschichtliches Bewußtsein*), the meta-consciousness that our historical consciousness is unavoidably conditioned by our own historicity (cf. "Circle," p. 78). Positivism is characterized by the *lack* of such meta-consciousness; it is instead the pursuit of "the phantom of a historical object, the topic of linearly advancing research" ("On the Circle," p. 78).[47]

---

[47]A common English translation of '*wirkungsgeschichtliches Bewußtsein*' has been 'effective-historical consciousness'. This rendition has the disadvantages of making it appear as if the German '*Wirkung*' (literally 'influence', 'effect', 'impact') were meant to have adjectival force and the consciousness to be historically effective. Gadamer intended neither implication. Admittedly his notion is a complex one, referring to the

"On the Circle of Understanding" thus ends with a criticism of positivism, and Gadamer contrasts with it the 'consciousness of the history of influence' which includes the awareness of a certain unity between reader and text. In *Wahrheit und Methode* the development of this line of thought leads immediately to the introduction of the related notions of the 'hermeneutical situation', or perspective, of the reader, and the 'horizon' which encloses any such perspective. German Romanticism warned against imputing, as reader, one's own horizon to the text; but taking this seriously brings with it the temptation to assume that there are always two separable horizons, the reader's and the text's. Gadamer, however, argues in effect that this assumption is merely another form of positivist historicism, as if the horizon of the past could be separated out and studied with scientific detachment. But just as there is no ontological separation of reader and text, so too there is no ultimate duality of horizons. 'Consciousness of the history of influence' is the awareness that, however different the text may be, our reading of it is condi-

---

reader's (or scholar's) awareness, during the confrontation with the text, of *the reality* (i.e., influence) *of history—in particular the text's own history of interpretation—in his/her own prejudices*. To understand what Gadamer is doing it is crucial to see that he does not regard the text and its *Wirkung* as merely contingently (e.g., causally) related. The text's influence consists in its being understood (and thus 'self-applied') by various generations of readers. This process is not accidental for the text: "Understanding is never a subjective attitude towards a given 'object', but instead belongs to the history of influence, i.e., *to the being* of what is understood" (Gadamer, 1960/1975, p. xix/xix). A Wittgensteinian might say that reading a text (in the way specific to each language-game) belongs to the structure of the language-games within which various kinds of texts *are constituted*. The intended contrast, in the context of the final paragraph of "On the Circle," is apparently with a (positivistic) *self*-forgetful, 'historical consciousness', i.e., one which is unaware of its own prejudices. (We are grateful to Ulrich Steinvorth and Hans Vaget for helpful suggestions on the translation of this vexed term. For more on the topic, as well as further references, see J. Weinsheimer, 1985, pp. 181–82, especially footnote 42.)

tioned by our own historicity. That is, every genuine understanding represents a "fusion of such allegedly independent horizons."[48]

In this volume Gadamer employs the concept of the horizon in his own literary-critical interpretation of Rainer Maria Rilke's *Duino Elegies* (essay 2). The polemical contention of this essay is that several major interpretations of the *Elegies* had not managed to get beyond *their own* horizons. Since one can only proceed from one's own standpoint, there is "a constant seduction to read and hear out of the text that which most willingly complies with one's own preconceptions," whether these preconceptions concern the substance of the poems (as in the case of Romano Guardini, 1953) or their form (as with Jakob Steiner, 1962). *Gadamer rejects both sorts of reading*, the first on the grounds that it violates the "canon of understanding given by the coherence of the sense of the whole" ("Rilke," p. 80), whereas the second is apparently rejected as a 'muddle of method'. What is in fact required, we are told, is that the interpreter give "Rilke's poetic language . . . a clarification of the horizon which encloses it" (p. 81). This in turn is only possible if we "start from [a] fore-understanding—forced upon us by the poetry itself—of what is spoken of," i.e., the subject matter (p. 83).[43]

This notion of a horizon is, we contend, of major importance for evaluation of the question whether there is any serious sense in which the humanities can plausibly be said to be autonomous. For the notion clarifies Gadamer's anti-positivist remarks, on p. 78 of "Circle," about the "phantom of a historical object." A critic of Gadamer might respond to those remarks (as Stegmüller in effect does) in this sort of way:

> When Gadamer speaks of an 'object', he apparently has in mind what positivist philosophy of science meant: some-

---

[48]Gadamer, 1960/1975, p. 289/273.

[49]Thus Gadamer's own procedure in "Rilke" rebuts the criticism that he offers no hint of the grounds on which an interpretation might be rationally *rejected*, and that hence he depicts literary interpretation as 'arbitrary'.

thing which is 'out there', quite independent of any subjective awareness of it, and which is the same no matter who is observing it or when it is being observed. The counterpart of the object on the side of the observer is method: by the use of the proper method a correct characterization of the object is eventually obtained, whether the object in question be a text (in the humanities) or a physical object, event, or process (in the natural sciences). Gadamer criticizes this conception on the grounds that it ignores the role in hermeneutical disciplines of the readers' historically inherited prejudices in constituting the 'object'. However, even before "On the Circle" was written, the thesis of the theory-ladenness of observation had won widespread acceptance. One result of this is that on the issue of the inevitability of observer-prejudice there is today something approaching general agreement, and therefore little or no distinction can be drawn between the humanities and the natural sciences.

Even if this is so, however, it says nothing to rule out distinctions at levels other than that of 'objectivity vs. subjectivity'. Gadamer can substantially concede this point about the 'object' and still contend that the concept of the 'fusion of horizons' brings out a unique feature of understanding in humanistic disciplines, to wit that they are concerned first and foremost with meaning, and thus—in the dialectic of *sich in der Sache verstehen*[50]—*with the self-understanding* of the reader. We will attempt in our Conclusion to offer a non-metaphorical reconstruction of Gadamer's central thesis of undecidability, and try to show how it is connected with this topic of self-understanding.

2.2 Stegmüller on Hermeneutics and Astronomy

Wolfgang Stegmüller's essay represents an attempt to 'rationally reconstruct' the autonomy thesis, i.e., the claim that

---

[50]Cf. note 44, above.

the 'hermeneutical circle' of the mutual interdependence of part and whole is *insuperable*, hence the process of interpretation is endless; and that this fact *methodologically* distinguishes the humanities from the natural sciences, for in the natural sciences hypotheses are decided once and for all. Stegmüller's attempt at reconstruction is, however, unsuccessful: none of the more precise reformulations he considers leads to a verification of the thesis of the methodological autonomy of the humanities.

Stegmüller's use of the tool of rational reconstruction marks his considerations as belonging to the philosophical tradition of logical empiricism. It is characteristic of this tradition to hold that the source of philosophical problems lies in their obscure or insufficiently precise linguistic expression. Rational reconstruction is the tool of choice for the solution, by means of clarification and conceptual reformulation, of philosophical problems in this sense.[51]

Since Stegmüller's attempted reconstruction of the 'hermeneutical principle' is a failure, another thesis, that of the 'unity of science', takes the place of the autonomy thesis at the close of his exposition. Here too one sees the legacy of logical empiricism. However, the thesis is given a new justification: a correct understanding of the natural sciences shows *them* to be more like the humanities than the philosophers of the Vienna Circle had suspected.

Stegmüller's text can be divided into four major sections: First, following some introductory historical remarks (pp. 102–4), he refers critically to a series of basic difficulties which one encounters in dealing with the literature of philosophical hermeneutics (pp. 104–10). Secondly he analyzes 'hermeneutical circle' in a number of different meanings of this term (pp. 110–19). Since in each case the object turns out to be problematical, he speaks here of 'dilemmas'. To speak in this manner of a 'dilemma' rules out from the start the notion that the

[51]On the concept of rational reconstruction see W. Stegmüller, 1970/1977, pp. 1–61.

hermeneutical circle is a logical (or 'vicious') circle (except in the case of the theoretical circle, where this danger does in fact threaten, pp. 115–16).

Thirdly, Stegmüller illustrates two of these dilemmas by comparing two case studies, the interpretation of Walther von der Vogelweide's poem of dream-love, on the one hand, and the discovery and interpretation of quasars on the other (pp. 119–30).

Fourthly, he presents his own thesis, one which he revised from an earlier and much shorter version of this paper:[52] based on appearances one might conclude that there is indeed a genuine difference between the humanities and the natural sciences, to wit only in the latter can we sharply distinguish between facts and so-called 'background knowledge' (p. 130). Although Stegmüller himself drew this conclusion in the earlier version, he rejects it here as illusory (pp. 133 ff.): to draw the 'sharp distinction' just mentioned is as little possible in the natural sciences as in the humanities. Thus the attempt rationally to reconstruct the notion of the hermeneutical circle proves futile, and the autonomy thesis collapses (pp. 149, 152).

In the second of the four parts of his essay Stegmüller distinguishes a number of dilemmas, each corresponding to a different possible sense of 'hermeneutical circle', and thus each representing a potential criterion for distinguishing between the humanities and the natural sciences: if the circle of part and whole could be demonstrated, in one or another of these senses, to be truly 'insuperable', the humanities would thereby be shown to have a unique 'circle-structure'. It turns out, however, that only in the case of the last two dilemmas is

[52]The original version was presented in 1972 at the German Philosophical Congress in Kiel (see Stegmüller, 1973b). This version was also published in English, "The So-Called Circle of Understanding," Stegmüller, 1977, vol. 2. The later and greatly expanded version which we have translated for this present volume plainly shows the results of Stegmüller's further reflection during the 1970s on the question of the autonomy thesis.

there even the appearance of support for the distinction in question.

The first two candidates Stegmüller characterizes as 'dilemmas of interpretation', the first in the case of *one's own* language, the second in the case of *foreign* languages. The former arises from the fact that it can sometimes be impossible to test an interpretive hypothesis on a text, because the text only becomes intelligible on the basis of the hypothesis. But of course this dilemma is serious only where the possibility of confirmatory evidence is limited to the text *alone*, which is hardly ever the case. In any event we are not confronted with a 'dilemma-in-principle', but rather with one which depends on whether we have more or less information, and the dilemma is to that extent eliminable. Were this otherwise, were this dilemma in fact insuperable, then what would follow would be the impossibility of the humanities rather than a characterization of their uniqueness.[53]

If the text is composed in a foreign language, the second dilemma *can* arise (but does not have to): it can happen that, say, historical texts can be understood only from the context of their epochs, whereas the epochs are accessible only through the texts. Once again, if we agree that information about the epoch can be gained from sources other than texts, the difficulty is seen to be one of degree, not of principle. As dilemmas of interpretation both these difficulties are found only in the humanities, but formally they have this structure: "In order to understand A, one would first have to understand B;—to acquire knowledge about B, one would first have to understand A." *In this form* both dilemmas no longer single out the humanities; in principle they can also turn up in other branches of learning.

From what has been said it follows that these dilemmas of interpretation a) are often capable of solution, and b)—given

[53]Stegmüller here (and throughout) simply *assumes* that the decidability of interpretations is a necessary condition for the humanities to be serious scholarly disciplines, an assumption which rests, as we shall see, upon his realist semantics.

the correctness of the formal reconstruction—are unsuited to be criteria for marking off the humanities.

The third possible candidate for what is meant by 'the hermeneutical circle' is the *theoretical circle*, which arises in cases where a certain sort of theoretical concept ('theoretical function concepts') can only be characterized as applying to individual cases provided that successful applications of the theory have *already* been made (pp. 115 f.). However this dilemma was uncovered precisely in the case of theories in the natural sciences, thus it too is as unsuited as the first two dilemmas to be a criterion for the autonomy of the humanities.[54]

Stegmüller introduces two distinct versions of the fourth dilemma, that of the *standpoint-dependence of the observer* (pp. 116–19). According to the first version 'hermeneutical circle' could mean that interpreters always bring to the text a definite pre-understanding, a decisive portion of which is supposed to be unexaminable. Accordingly interpreters cannot free themselves from *these* presuppositions. On Stegmüller's view this thesis is burdened with two problems. First, he finds here a confusion of "unexaminable in principle" with "not yet in fact examined": of course every process of reasoning takes its start from definite presuppositions, but at least one by one each of these is capable of examination (and thus, where appropriate, correction). We cannot conclude from the fact that we always reason on the basis of presuppositions that there are presuppositions unexaminable in principle. Stegmüller notes here that in any event the hermeneuticist has to carry the burden of proof for the existence of such unexaminable presuppositions—and what would such a proof look like?

We hasten to comment that Stegmüller fails in this case to do full justice to the dilemma. In its fully developed form the

[54]Stegmüller is relying here on a reconstruction by J. D. Sneed, 1971, of Kuhn's philosophy of science, a reconstruction which Stegmüller clarifies in more detail in other writings. Cf. in particular his 1969–73, volume II, subvolume 2. This subvolume has appeared in English (Stegmüller, 1976).

dilemma says: we can be sure the text is understood properly only when the assumptions on which the interpretation is based are completely visible; but certain of the interpreter's presuppositions are tacit not in that they (say, for the sake of economy of argumentation) simply have not been expressed, but instead because they are *not conscious*, have not been made explicit in the encounter with the text. Thus one may first of all respond to Stegmüller that every pre-judgement can of course be criticized *once it has been identified*. Just this identification, however, is what is missing for crucial presuppositions. Secondly, we lack a criterion for saying when indeed *all* presuppositions are allowed to count as unproblematical (or examined) in view of the fact that such presuppositions constitute a tacit, nonexplicit realm, i.e., a realm that is not fully open to view.

This response might seem to rebound back against the hermeneuticist. For if the pre-judgments in question are hidden, how then—Stegmüller's challenge is quite right—is their existence to be proved? Here Gadamer's answer is: from a distance. From our historical standpoint we perceive the conceptual horizons of others with their tacit pre-judgments. Furthermore, as we noted above, when in the confrontation with the text our prejudice of perfection is disturbed, we can, through *self*-distancing, become aware of our own prejudices.

As for the second version of the fourth dilemma, 'standpoint' could be understood in the Kuhnian sense, i.e., as 'paradigm'. Be that as it may, Kuhn's philosophy of science was of course developed to apply to the natural sciences. Thus the notion of a paradigm can hardly serve to establish the autonomy of the humanities.

Stegmüller presents the two remaining dilemmas jointly: the *dilemma of confirmation* and that of *distinguishing background knowledge from knowledge of facts* (pp. 119 ff.). He illustrates these dilemmas with a comparison of two case studies, the debate in German studies over the meaning of a poem by Walther von der Vogelweide ("Nemt, frowe, disen Kranz"), and the discussion in astronomy of the nature of quasars.

In what do these two dilemmas consist? We have a dilemma of confirmation when, faced with facts to be explained, we are unable to decide, on the basis of the available information, between two competing hypotheses: every argument in favor can be countered with an argument against. Stegmüller is able to show that each of the two debates he discusses has the form of this sort of dilemma.

What Stegmüller calls the problem of distinguishing background knowledge from knowledge of facts represents, so to speak, the other side of the coin from the dilemma of confirmation. It arises when background knowledge and knowledge of facts fuse to such an extent that the facts are no longer able to serve as judge over our interpretations. Stegmüller characterizes this fusion as the "theory-ladenness of observation." His overlapping consideration of these two dilemmas (V and VI) is extremely complicated. The complications are in part due to the incomplete reworking of his original thesis (see note 52, above). In the original text (Stegmüller, 1973b) he reaches the tentative conclusion that there 'seems' to be a way of differentiating methodologically between the humanities and the natural sciences, since only in the latter can we draw a sharp boundary between background knowledge and facts. He retains this tentative conclusion in the present version of the essay (p. 130) while at the same time developing the opposite conclusion that there is *no* methodological difference between the two branches of knowledge. (p. 149)

In the natural sciences it *seems prima facie* possible to separate factual from background knowledge, since in this case the latter sort of knowledge is apparently exclusively nomological, whereas background knowledge in the humanities is apparently not nomological. Thus an exact separation of background and factual knowledge in the humanities becomes possible only on the basis of a different supposition, to wit that the humanities deal with pure, uninterpreted facts, while the background knowledge on which they draw is hypothetical (pp. 135 f.). However, Stegmüller points out that there is general agreement today that, on the whole, factual knowledge itself is hypothetical, and he buttresses his point with a semantical argument derived from Putnam. Thus, up to this point, it looks as though a sharp distinction between background and factual knowledge would be possible only in the natural sciences, hence dilemma VI apparently gives us a unique characteristic of the humanities. Stegmüller would seem to have established the thesis that the humanities *are*, in some sense, autonomous.

However, not only the thesis of the purity and uninterpreted character of experience (applied especially to the humanities in the course of this argument) needs revision. So too does the thesis—developed now more fully—that the background knowledge of the natural scientist contains only nomic statements (pp. 147 ff.). Stegmüller argues that even in the natural sciences there is no sharp distinction to be drawn between factual and background knowledge. Thus on this issue there is shown to be no difference at all between the humanities and the natural sciences. The sixth dilemma cannot be remedied; it is to some extent 'insuperable', but it applies to both branches of knowledge.

In summation: none of the six possible interpretations of 'hermeneutical circle' which Stegmüller considers yields convincing grounds for a differentiation of the humanities from the natural sciences. We noted above that Stegmüller ends his investigation by arguing for the methodological unity of the sciences. We can now see more clearly that this result rests upon a conception of the natural sciences which assumes neither uninterpreted data of experience nor any sharp distinction between background and factual knowledge. *Under this ('post-positivistic') conception* these sciences cannot be methodologically distinguished from the humanities.[55]

---

[55]As C. Taylor has pointed out, M. Hesse and R. Rorty have argued for a "new thesis of the unity of science," to wit that "all sciences are equally hermeneutic" (C. Taylor, 1980, p. 26). Taylor sees this thesis as following necessarily from the surrender of the empiricist conception of natural science. Rorty agrees: "The demise of logical empiricism means that there is no interesting split between the *Natur-* and the *Geisteswissenschaften*" (Rorty, 1980, p. 39). According to Rorty's pre-

What this shows in turn is that the traditional autonomy thesis of hermeneuticists such as Dilthey made use of a *positivistic* conception of the natural sciences. This conception rested on a particular description (one now recognized as inadequate) of how natural science proceeds, to wit by testing nomic hypotheses against uninterpreted observation reports. Following Kuhn and Putnam, Stegmüller rejects this concep-

---

sentation in *Philosophy and the Mirror of Nature*, however, there is an important difference between 'epistemology' and 'hermeneutics'. To proceed epistemologically is, according to Rorty, to presuppose that all discourse (at least "every discourse on a given topic") shares "the objects to be confronted by the mind, or the rules which constrain inquiry . . . " (Rorty, 1979, pp. 315–16). According to epistemology, "all contributions to a given discourse are commensurable" in this sense, that they are "able to be brought under a set of rules which will tell us how rational agreement can be reached on what would settle the issue on every point where statements seem to conflict" (ibid., p. 316). Thus all contributions to a given discourse must be translatable into a 'correct' and common terminology. 'Hermeneutic' procedure, on the other hand, does not presuppose the commensurability of all discourse, but instead, refusing to translate, is "willing to pick up the jargon of the interlocutor" (Rorty, 1979, p. 318). Whether one proceeds hermeneutically or epistemologically is purely a question of *familiarity* with the given discourse: "We will be epistemological where we understand perfectly well what is happening but want to codify it in order to extend, or strengthen, or teach, or 'ground' it. We must be hermeneutical where we do not understand what is happening but are honest enough to admit it, rather than being *blatantly* 'Whiggish' about it" (Rorty, 1979, p. 321). Rorty regards his distinction of epistemology and hermeneutics as a generalization of Thomas Kuhn's notions of 'normal' and 'revolutionary' science. In particular Rorty extends these notions to the *Geisteswissenschaften*: there is "no difficulty getting commensuration in theology or morals or literary criticism when these areas of culture are 'normal'. At certain periods, it has been as easy to determine which critics have a 'just perception' of the value of a poem as it is to determine which experimenters are capable of making accurate observations and precise measurements" (Rorty, 1979, p. 322). Thus hermeneutics and epistemology each have a place in both the natural sciences *and* the humanities, and it is external factors—for instance, the historical period—that decide which mode of inquiry predominates.

tion of the natural sciences in favor of one according to which the natural sciences, like the humanities, rest on theory-laden foundations.

This result corresponds to our remarks above on constructivism and interpretation (pp. 16–27). There we noted the widespread agreement in twentieth-century German philosophy that neither a text nor a fact of nature can ever count as definitively understood, and noted that, among philosophers who reject the thesis of the undecidability of interpretations, some adopt a view of the *de facto* interminability (or undecid*edness*) of interpretation which comes close to the undecid*ability* thesis. (above, p. 26) In this connection we mentioned Hilary Putnam. We want now to expand on those remarks. Putnam's realist theory of meaning includes the contention that the meaning of most descriptive terms consists *inter alia* in the nontheoretical referent of the term *plus* a theory-dependent 'stereotype' made up of a series of beliefs, individual or communal, about the object(s) designated by the term in question.[56] A consequence of Putnam's approach is that *no matter how we use* a concept, its referent and, hence, meaning are fixed all along. Applied to propositions this means that their truth-conditions are settled, and hence the propositions themselves are true or false, whether or not we are (yet, or even ever) in a position to determine their truth-value. Were the truth-conditions not settled, the proposition would simply have no determinate meaning.

Stegmüller makes use of Putnam's theory of meaning in order to show that our language is always theory-laden, never a 'pure' report of experience. A "dilemma of distinguishing background knowledge from knowledge of facts" (above, pp. 42–43) follows directly from Putnam's theory: there is *no* theory-neutral judge of our interpretations. Thus central to Stegmüller's account of the endlessness of debate in both the natural sciences and the humanities is the notion that the

---

[56]See H. Putnam, "The Meaning of 'Meaning'," in Putnam, 1975–1983.

hypotheses which constitute our stereotypes are always fallible. Even if we should chance to hit upon the true stereotype, we would not be in a position to realize it with certainty. Thus for Stegmüller, to characterize interpretations (or explanations) as 'undecidable' is in effect to point to a largely practical problem, that the evidence which would decide the matter is unavailable to us. Nonetheless it does exist, a decision is conceivable. An omniscient being would have no more trouble deciding on the truth-value of an interpretation than it would on the truth-value of hypotheses concerning, for example, other minds, the distant past, or the spatially remote.

Applied to the kind of literary-critical question which Stegmüller examines, his thesis of the methodological equality of literary studies and astronomy is convincing. For his case studies show that in both disciplines there are questions which are a) decidable in principle, but b) only relative to accepted stereotypes ('relative decidability').[57] However, it must be pointed out that Stegmüller's contention goes further, to the claim that *all* interpretive disputes in the humanities are every bit as decidable in principle—relative to a given stereotype—as disputes in the natural sciences. The *prima facie* plausibility of this contention is enhanced by the fact that the literary-critical disagreement which he discusses in such detail is one which everyone would agree to call decidable in principle. The disagreement between the two Germanists, Wapnewski and Hahn,—which Stegmüller describes as turning on the correct ordering of two stanzas in Walther von der Vogelweide's poem—depends in fact on the intention of the poet and hence is one that could be settled (if for example we were to discover an *authoritative* fourteenth-century manu-

[57]A simple example of a question that is 'relatively decidable' would be this: given our stereoptype for the term 'gold' we can decide whether a piece of metal is gold or not. Nonetheless, since stereotypes are fallible and subject to change with the advance of science, our decision may well turn out to be wrong; and furthermore, we *can never know* for sure whether we are right!

script). For who would dispute the author's right to determine the order of the verses in his or her poem?

Stegmüller's chosen example turns on the fact that in literary studies there are issues which can, at least in principle, be decided by appeal to the author's intention. Thus both in literary studies and the natural sciences there are indeed 'relatively decidable' questions. But to be complete, Stegmüller's critique of the autonomy thesis would seem to have required treatment of the kind of literary-critical disagreement discussed by Specht, i.e., one in which each of the conflicting interpretations construes the text in the light of its own background. That Stegmüller does not feel the need to discuss such a case can, we contend, be explained thus: given his explicit reliance on a realist semantics, there is for him *no such thing* as a meaningful interpretation which is *in principle* undecidable. To call a proposition p undecidable in principle is to say that it has *no determinate truth-conditions*, which for a realist amounts to saying that p has no fixed meaning.

It is important to distinguish the type of undecidability which Specht discusses (and which we will claim is central to literary criticism) from two other types:

1) the undecidability of hypotheses in science—because of the problem of induction, on the one hand, and the logical status of hypotheses (Duhem, Quine, et al.) on the other, neither the truth nor the falsity of scientific hypotheses is provable, and in this sense they are undecidable. A Quinean might apply the same lesson to literary and even psychoanalytic interpretations, claiming that the text itself (which might, as in the psychoanalytic case, include behavior) can neither prove nor refute an interpretation; and

2) undecidability because of the paradigm-relativity of evidence—it is possible to decide between two competing hypotheses only where a neutral court of appeals (e.g., common observational evidence) is available, which is by no means always the case. In the case of interpretations one could argue that the text by no means represents the neutral tribunal by appeal to which one interpretation could be chosen over another. Taken together, these two types of undecidability can

of course be added to the well-known Kuhnian problem of scientific rationality: neither can we show that a paradigm itself is true (or false), nor can we prove that one paradigm is nearer the truth than another.

Both sorts of undecidability are distinct from what we ourselves mean by the term in this Introduction. We are not concerned with the problem of induction, nor with logical immunity from falsification, nor with the sort of undecidability which results when the requisite proof is missing. For all these reasons one might call interpretations undecidable. But our thesis is that even if we had access to *all* the facts, and even if complete agreement were to reign among literary critics on the 'correct' paradigm (if all were New Critics, say, or Structuralists), interpretations would still be undecidable. For in fact we have no idea what it would mean for a literary interpretation to be true (or false). As we will argue below, it is the *notion of proof* itself, of establishing something as true or false, which *de facto* has no place in the language-game of literary criticism.

Thus Specht's notion of 'undecidability in principle' introduces considerations which, if correct, tend to undermine Stegmüller's central thesis of the unity of science. Furthermore, they do so by introducing a different conception of meaning and without sliding back to an outmoded conception of natural science.

2.3 'Constructive' Interpretations vs. Hypotheses

On Specht's view, *all* interpretations, whether of texts or other data, contain an element of *subjective stipulation* (or decision), for we speak of 'interpretation' only where compelling evidence for one or another explanation of the phenomenon is lacking. 'Subjective stipulation' does not, of course, mean 'complete arbitrariness': any interpretation worth its salt will be based on reasons, arguments, evidence of one sort or another. Nonetheless the evidence offered in support of the interpretation is not (or not yet) sufficient to convince all (or most) of the relevant practitioners (e.g., the paleontologists, in the case which Specht cites from Erben, 1975).

Early in his essay Specht introduces a watershed distinction. Many interpretations of data (including texts) are in principle *decidable* (relative to the ruling paradigm), i.e., the available evidence would be sufficient, once marshalled, to establish one of the competing interpretations as correct. For example, the astronomer Le Verrier interpreted the observable disturbances in Uranus' orbit as being caused by the gravitational pull of a planet whose orbit is outside that of Uranus. This interpretation was neatly verified by Galle's discovery of Neptune in 1846. Such interpretations, verifiable (or falsifiable) in principle, Specht calls 'hypotheses'.

According to Specht, some literary-critical interpretations (those that aim at discovering the author's intention) are no less hypotheses than the interpretations of the geologists, i.e., their truth-value can in principle be decided. However, not all literary interpretations have the epistemological status of hypotheses. Specht also speaks of 'constructive', that is, undecidable, interpretations. As example he offers three attempts to clarify the meaning of "Anniversary," a short lyric by the German poet Stefan George. Each of the attempts results in a reading which, though supported by the text, is inconsistent with the other readings.

This situation, familiar to all literary critics, is for the 'objectivists' among them (see above, p. 25) one which should not be called 'insuperable'. Were it insuperable, it would constitute a *prima facie* threat to the claim of literary studies to be a serious, objective discipline (what would, in Germany, be called a '*Wissenschaft*').

When Specht speaks of a 'constructive interpretation', he plainly has none of the 'objectivist' positions (author-intentional, text-intentional, et al.) in mind. He regards it as a common occurrence that

> neither the author's intention nor the text so determine the sense of . . . [a] poem that we could give this sense in a true proposition. (p. 160)

But why not? "Surely," one would like to respond, "*Stefan George* knew whether he meant, for example, one bridegroom or two. Even if we concede that the 'text intention' is often ambiguous, in many cases the author will have had just one of the potential meanings in mind. If we are able to determine that intention, does that not settle the question of the text's meaning?"

Specht's answer here is curious, for he seems to regard it as the prerogative *of the author* to determine whether or not an interpretation should aim at determining his or her intention:

> the correctness of the interpretation in these cases [in which critics aim "precisely *not* at the author's intention"] cannot consist in a correspondence of interpretation and author's intention. This is especially so when authors themselves do not claim for their intentions the status of the exclusive and true sense of their texts. (p. 159, emphasis added)

But it is hard to see how an individual author could have the power to determine that the meaning of his/her poem consists in the author's intention, rather than in something else. Surely the meaning of the phrase "meaning of a poem," like that of "anthracite coal" or any other term, is not a matter of the speaker's personal preference. On this point the major semantic theories, whether realist or constructivist, are in agreement.

Specht's main reason for holding that some literary-critical interpretations are 'constructive' is, we suspect, given in the unobtrusive clause which precedes the statement just quoted:

> But many literary critical interpretations *aim precisely not* at the author's intention, so that the correctness, etc. (ibid.)[58]

---

[58]Emphasis added. The logic of Specht's position, we note, applies equally to the notion of the (unique) 'text-intention'. 'Unique', incidentally, does not exclude ambiguity in this case. An everyday utterance, for example, can be ambiguous because the speaker intends it to be so. In that case it has a single correct interpretation, namely the one which captures the intended ambiguities. Such an interpretation is not 'constructive'.

The basic idea is apparently this: it is *de facto* the practice of the literary-critical community not (or, at least, not in every kind of case) to regard the author's intention as the measure of a correct reading. Even in cases where this intention has been quite reliably determined, there is nothing like unanimity among the critics that the correct interpretation, i.e., one which makes the best sense of the text, has *ipso facto* been found.[59] An 'objectivist' metacritic is likely to counter that critics who do not take into account the author's authority are simply *mistaken*, just as a geologist who did not take into account the plain fossil evidence would be mistaken. Specht does not consider such an objection, but he might respond in this fashion: one can speak of a 'mistake' only where there are *de facto* norms governing the activity in question. As geology is presently practiced, the fossil record is accorded a weighty authority. Hence it makes sense to ascribe a mistake to a geologist who does not take into account such evidence. But the situation is different in literary criticism, the author's authority does not hold the same sort of undisputed position as does the fossil record in geology. Hence one cannot say, "Measured by the norms of literary-critical practice, not to take into account the author's interpretation is a mistake."

Specht's alternative is to draw a distinction between 'decidable' and 'constructive' interpretations in literary criticism. The former are hypotheses, a decision on their correctness is possible in principle. Not so in the case of 'constructive' interpretations. There the critic must decide "to accept one of the possible readings, thereby clearly fixing the sense of the text only in the act of interpretation" (p. 160). This distinction gives us a new perspective on Stegmüller's treatment of the dispute over Walther's lyric. From a Spechtian perspective the issue of the correct order of the stanzas is plainly decidable (at least in principle): only the poet can set the order of his or her text. But other issues are just as plainly not decidable:

---

[59]One such case, concerning E. R. Wasserman's author-intentional reading of the final couplet of Keats's "Ode on a Grecian Urn," is discussed in Connolly, 1986.

i) the question of whether the dream-love lyric is a pastoral (as Wapnewski, 1957, contended) is not one which can be settled by appeal to the author's intention or any other objective evidence. Once one has acknowledged that Walther's poem has some, but not all, of the features which have traditionally been regarded as constitutive or essential for pastorals, then the interpreter's decision to regard the poem as a pastoral *is at the same time* the acknowledgment of a definite set of criteria as operative for such classification. It is not as if one *discovers* that particular characteristics of a poem, say an accentuated difference of estate between a knight and a country lass,[60] are essential marks of pastoral poetry. Rather, the interpreter who thinks there *are* such discoverable characteristics and on this basis insists that, come what may, Walther's lyric *cannot* be a pastoral (since it lacks them, or some of them) is led astray by the fact that what appears to be a deep empirical insight into the essence of pastoral poetry represents in fact the *decision* to use these characteristics as definitional. The proposition, "This poem cannot be a pastoral, since it does not accentuate the difference of estate," conceals its own deeper meaning, to wit: "I will [or perhaps: let us] regard as pastorals only poems in which differences of estate are accentuated;"

ii) furthermore, questions of the overall interpretation of the meaning (*Sinn*) of a poem, an issue which seems clearly to belong to the second, 'constructive' category, are not given a separate discussion by Stegmüller.

Having tried out his categories on the field of literary criticism, Specht proceeds to apply them to psychoanalytic interpretations. He presents a detailed example, a forgotten appointment, which is then given a psychoanalytic reading as a 'slip'. We speak here of 'interpretation' rather than 'explanation' because, says Specht, "the rules for applying the individual concepts [of psychoanalytic theory] are not so precisely laid down that we can clearly and objectively decide in each

[60]See Stegmüller, essay 3, pp. 124–25.

case whether or not the concept should be applied" (p. 164). As a result, our explanatory efforts retain a provisional character which calls for the stipulative element typical of interpretations.

But *what kind* of interpretation do we have in this sort of case: decidable? or 'constructive'? Many psychoanalysts have in effect assumed or argued that the former is the case, and anyone who has undergone a successful analysis is likely to regard the analyst's interpretations as conclusively verified. But Specht rejects this point of view, since an analytic interpretation relies for its support on evidence which "must itself first be interpreted psychoanalytically" (p. 166); in particular, the direct testimony of the patient about his or her *unconscious* wishes or fears is itself an interpretation which, as things stand, cannot be decisively verified or falsified.

Hence there is, Specht contends, a suggestive analogy between analytic interpretations and 'constructive' interpretations in literary criticism: in both cases what the subject (author or patient) says is not taken as either a verification or a falsification of the interpretation. He argues that this no more impugns the 'serious' or 'scientific' character of the one kind of interpretation than of the other. In each case the subjective element can, in principle, be kept under control. In psychoanalysis this is the aim of 'counter-transference analysis' (p. 168), in which the analyst is sensitized to his or her own unconscious material which, left unchecked, can easily distort the manner in which he or she interprets the patient's material. Once again we have a situation where one kind of psychoanalytic interpretation is used to validate or check another. On the other hand, as Specht concedes, the notion lingers that an unconscious wish might in some sense be, or be correlated with, a set of physical or neurophysiological 'hard facts' about the patient; and that at some time in the future of science an interpretation could be verified by appeal to those facts. But this is an issue whose full discussion Specht leaves for another occasion (p. 169).[61]

---

[61]One should note that there seems to be a certain development in Specht's published views on the question. In Specht, 1981, he accounts

Specht also refuses to enter into a discussion of "the exceedingly difficult, and thusfar by no means solved, problem of the hermeneutical circle" (p. 166). Hence he makes no connection between that problem and his notion of 'constructive' interpretation. But there are such connections to be made, in particular in answer to those who may wonder *what use* there

---

for the undecidability of dream-interpretations in a manner different from that in which he here explains the undecidability of the interpretation of a slip. In the 1981 piece he writes: " . . . dream-interpretations can be decisively confirmed by recourse neither to the dream itself and the [dreamer's] free associations, nor to [his or her] conscious intentions" (p.83). And: "We can never verify our interpretations by asking the dreamer" (p. 77). In the present piece, on the other hand, his account rests on the claim that in psychoanalysis there is no process of verification independent of psychoanalytic theory. Furthermore it is only in the earlier piece that Specht suggests we regard psychoanalytic interpretations as recommendations. To regard interpretations in Specht's fashion is to understand a dreamer, for example, as someone who *could have had* a certain unconscious wish, in the light of which supposition the dreamer attains a new and fruitful self-perspective. This amounts to the instrumentalist view that psychoanalysis is a tool for behavioral modification or for changing the psychic orientation of the patient or client, quite independently of the descriptive content of the analyst's underlying etiological hypothesis. The question of what "really happened" in the patient's or client's past is *suspended*. In addition to Specht a number of other recent authors have advanced similar views, e.g., G. Klein, 1976, R. Schafer, 1976, and P. Ricoeur, 1981.

A. Grünbaum, 1984, has produced a recent criticism of this instrumentalist approach. However, although he pinpoints many questionable points in the views of the individual 'hermeneuticists' (Ricoeur, Habermas, et al.), he seems to have no argument against the logical possibility of an instrumentalistically construed psychoanalysis, other than that it is untrue to Freud's intentions. The main alternative to instrumentalism is to defend the historical, etiological content of psychological interpretations. But this step, as we shall see below, would not once and for all clarify the status of such interpretations, since historical claims themselves belong, according to M. Dummett, to that broad class of statements which are not decidable. In the light of Dummett's criticisms of 'semantic realism' we will find reason to question the deeply ingrained insistence that if interpretations are to be rationally assessible, they must be decidable.

can be in giving, in literary studies, a 'constructive' interpretation (i.e., one whose truth or falsity cannot be definitively established). When an analyst encounters unexpected behavior from a patient, this can create a situation in which further progress in the analysis requires that *the analyst* re-examine his or her own presuppositions ('pre-judgments'). So too an 'eminent' text can force the critic to confront his or her hidden prejudgments. Surely the interpretation of literature does not have the same sort of purpose as depth psychology. Nonetheless if the central tenets of Gadamer's 'philosophical hermeneutics' are correct, then there is in fact a kind of analogy between the two. Literary studies, indeed the humanities in general, are not depth psychology, but they serve the function, according to Gadamer, of bringing to light *our* 'prejudices' as readers and critics about the issues of life, love, and death with which their eminent texts deal. Must we not concede that both the logical structure of interpretations in the humanistic disciplines and the self-knowledge which the pursuit of those disciplines requires mark them off from the natural sciences?

3. Conclusion: Undecidability and Self-Knowledge

Gadamer's and Specht's constructivist understanding of the *de facto* interminable stream of interpretations given to eminent texts plainly does not square with the attitude of most literary critics, whose straightforward intention is to uncover the (unique) meaning of the text by giving the uniquely true interpretation. In this conclusion we want to defend the view that underlying the dispute about the autonomy of hermeneutics is a disagreement about semantics: the theory of meaning which Stegmüller borrows from Putnam underlies this attitude of most literary critics. For 'semantic realism' implies the existence of that unique meaning which the interpreter sets out to find. From the standpoint of constructivism, however, realist semantics merely obscures the actual undecidability of a central kind of interpretation. The alternative to realism is constructivist semantics, and it underlies Gadamer's version of the autonomy thesis, his claim that the central point of the hermeneutical disciplines consists in a specific kind of self-knowledge, and that this point distinguishes them from the natural sciences.

Let us recapitulate the argument of this Introduction:

1.) Gadamer regards interpretations of 'eminent' texts as undecidable because each such interpretation takes place within the horizon of the interpreter's historically given prejudices, in the light of which the text itself is constituted. Thus the text cannot be viewed as an independent tribunal, 'theory-neutral' as it were, and capable of deciding on interpretations which derive from separate prejudice-horizons.

From this Gadamer inferred that the humanities are autonomous, for in the natural sciences the "object [of inquiry] can, at least ideally, be defined as what would be known in the completed science of nature."[62] But since the 'object of inquiry' in the humanities can only be constituted by the prejudice-structure of a given epoch, the notion of an idealized, epoch-independent definition of it makes no sense.

2.) Stegmüller objected that interpretations in the humanities and explanations in the natural sciences are equally undecidable. For the latter are no more concerned with the 'pure' data of experience than are the former with 'pure' texts that are simply there in front of one. Instead, observation statements in science always contain hypothetical components, hence what he calls the dilemmas of "confirmation" and of "distinguishing background knowledge from facts" cannot be escaped. As a result a differentiation of the natural sciences and the humanities cannot be justified on the grounds that the data are uninterpreted only in the latter.[63]

---

[62]Gadamer, 1960/1975, p. 269/253.

[63]As noted above, A. Grünbaum (1984) has also criticized the autonomy thesis (e.g., in the writings of Habermas and Ricoeur) for incorporating a false picture of the natural sciences. Habermas' views, he claims, suppose a "stone age physics" (p. 20), while Ricoeur is said to paint a false picture of academic psychology, which in fact proceeds in

Stegmüller buttresses his view that observational reports have hypothetical character by appealing to Putnam's philosophy of language, particularly the thesis that the meaning of most descriptive terms consists *inter alia* in the nontheoretical reference of the term *and* a theory-dependent 'stereotype' made up of a series of beliefs, individual or communal, about the object(s) designated by the term in question. Thus through the stereotype the observation language incorporates hypothetical elements in the form of beliefs about the designated object. These beliefs, however, can prove to be false, which rules out "our ever being able to employ the corresponding expressions to make absolutely certain statements."[64]

3.) Specht agrees with Gadamer that interpretations of the central kind in the humanities are undecidable. To be sure he admits (and Gadamer would certainly go along with him) that there are also decidable interpretations, e.g., those which aim explicitly at establishing the author's intention. On the other

---

the manner of a natural science (pp. 44 and 66). Whatever the faults of Habermas, Ricoeur, et al., Grünbaum seems to us to overlook the central question: is the undecidability of interpretation not of a quite different importance in the hermeneutical disciplines? and does not interpreting therefore play a fundamentally different role in hermeneutics, on the one hand, and natural science, on the other? We explore this question in detail below.

Let us make clear here that we share R. Rorty's view (above, pp. 43–44, note 55) that there are decidable and undecidable explanations or interpretations in *both* the humanities and the natural sciences. However, it does not, as far as we can see, follow that there are no essential differences in the two cases. For example, to regard literary-critical interpretations as decidable is not a question of the prevailing taste, but rather dogmatism or confused philosophy, which purveys a false picture of literary-critical activity. To turn Kuhn's terminology around: the undecidability of literary-critical interpretations is *normal* literary criticism, whereas decidability is the normal state of affairs in the natural sciences. This situation could not be reversed without fostering a very new conception of literary criticism (much as a new conception of natural science was born in the seventeenth century).

[64]Stegmüller, essay 3, below, pp. 137–38.

hand, he argues that in the natural sciences an important class of explanations, if not provable once and for all, are nonetheless taken as settled by the practitioners, i.e., treated as decided. This is—contra Stegmüller—quite different from the case of literary criticism.

Does all of this leave room for a thesis of the autonomy of the humanities? Our answer is: to some extent. Closer inspection shows that decidability and its contrary are assigned quite different values (or weights) in the two areas of learning. For in a natural science such as geology a question such as that about the age of certain fossils counts as decidable in principle, and establishing facts of this kind constitutes an important part of such disciplines. But in literary criticism decidable questions, such as those concerning the author's intention, are by no means reckoned as of central importance, since in the ongoing debate about the meaning *of the text* critics regularly overrule even the clearly expressed intention of the author. Thus one could say that, while decidable and undecidable interpretations mark *both* the natural sciences and the humanities, they are weighted within those disciplines in contrary ways: decidability is central in the sciences, undecidability in the humanities.

This much can be gleaned from a survey of the four essays collected in this volume. Nonetheless, as a resumé (not to mention as a new version of the autonomy thesis) this survey seems unsatisfactory. For it depends upon a characterization of the hermeneutical disciplines which contradicts the common self-understanding of their practitioners, who aim at producing not only interpretations which are nonarbitrary and well-founded, but also such as are *true*. This self-understanding (which denies the existence of undecidable interpretations) must be accounted for by any version of the autonomy thesis which bases the claim of autonomy on the putatively greater weight assigned to undecidable interpretations by those very practitioners!

This attitude of the literary critic can be traced back to a particular view of meaning which we have repeatedly labeled 'semantic realism': the meaning of a statement consists in its truth-conditions, which in turn consist of the possible states of affairs which obtain if the statement is true. Thus, to understand a statement is to know what would be the case if it were true. From this it follows that, corresponding to a literary text, there must be a particular possible state of affairs, the text's meaning, which would be the case were a given literary interpretation of that text true. According to one realist view this state of affairs is the author's intention, according to another it is the text-intention. Thus the true interpretation which the literary critic is pursuing aims precisely at the author's (or the text-) intention, i.e., the *unique* meaning of the text. To this extent realism is the semantical foundation of hermeneutical objectivism.

This realist underpinning reveals itself especially clearly when the critic, confronted with the history of the interpretation of an eminent text (and thus with a history of 'obsolete' interpretations), does not despair, but instead continues to search for the text's unique meaning. For according to the underlying semantical assumption, where there is (indeed must be) a unique meaning, all previous failures are merely temporary setbacks.

Constructivism criticizes this initial version of semantic realism, thus: the claim that the meaning of a proposition consists in its truth-conditions becomes ever harder to accept the further we move away from simple descriptions of things present to hand, e.g., to statements about the past or about the contents of other minds. "Janet believes that the cat is on the mat" and "The cat was on the mat last week" seem no more difficult to understand than "The cat is on the mat," but specifying the truth-conditions of such propositions is notoriously difficult.

Realists have a more sophisticated counter to this line of criticism: no matter *how we use* a concept, its reference and, hence, meaning are fixed all along. Applied to propositions this means that their truth-conditions are settled, and hence the propositions themselves true or false, whether or not we are in a position to state the truth-conditions and hence determine their truth-value. Putnam's theory of meaning, introduced by Stegmüller to show that even our observation-language is theory-laden, is of this more sophisticated kind, for according to it the referent of a term is, as we saw above (in section 2.2), fixed independently of the term's 'stereotype'.

The Achilles' heel of this approach lies in its corollary that, since meaning determines reference (the core notion of realism) while the stereotypes of speakers are fallible, we can never be sure that we understand the meanings of the terms we use. But is it sensible to claim that only an omniscient being could really understand English (or any other natural language)?

This is the point which Michael Dummett has doggedly pressed in his writings on realism and anti-realism. We need not be pushed to the corollary just stated, he has argued, because a quite different approach to meaning is available to us in the writings of Wittgenstein, an approach which takes the meaning of a proposition to consist not in its truth-conditions, but rather in its assertability-conditions, a quite different matter.[65] To understand, for instance, "The cat was on the mat last week," is to grasp not what would make it true, but rather the criteria which justify one in asserting it.[66]

---

[65]See for example Wittgenstein, 1969/1974, I, 40: "That which one understands as the justification of an assertion constitutes the meaning of the assertion" (our translation).

[66]Note that Putnam, impressed by Dummett's arguments, has somewhat altered his original theory. But in doing so he gives Dummett's approach an unusual twist by taking it to be a theory, not of meaning, but of truth, to wit that a proposition is *true* if its assertion is justified. Cf. Putnam's "Reference and Truth," pp. 83 ff., and "Introduction," pp. xvi f., in Putnam, 1975. But there seems to be no such pragmatic theory of truth in Dummett's thinking, since he acknowledges that a proposition can be warranted but false. Indeed the pragmatic theory would be diametrically opposed to the tendency of his argumentation, which leaves up in the air the question of the truth-value of certain warranted assertions. (Cf. his "Bringing About the Past," in Dummett, 1978.) By casting Dummett's approach in this manner Putnam serves his own interests, which include giving a theory of truth-as-"idealized justification," as opposed to justification based on "present evidence" (Putnam,

Dummett and others have illustrated the approach of constructivist semantics by applying it to philosophical issues which have proven difficult for realism, in particular assertions about the past and about other minds.[67] One is justified in asserting "She's in pain" of Jones, provided Jones manifests the appropriate behavior in the given circumstances. The behavior constitutes the assertability conditions; thus one explains the meaning of "x is in pain" by indicating the circumstances in which asserting it is justified. That one *understands* this statement is shown by the justification she or he would give for asserting it, e.g., "I say that Jones is in pain because she's groaning and ministering to that gash on her knee." The decisive difference between the constructivist and the realist approaches is that in its account of meaning the former makes no essential appeal to the concept of truth: it is obvious that the truth of the behavioral description does not allow us to *infer* the truth of the psychological statement: one can be fully justified in asserting such a statement and still be wrong.[68]

So too, according to constructivism, the meaning of an interpretation will also be explained by indicating the conditions which warrant its use in the language-game.[69] (By contrast, a realist would hold that the meaning of an interpre-

---

1975, p. xvii). For if truth were warranted assertability—the view that Putnam attributes (inaccurately, we contend) to Dummett—then every stereotype would correctly determine the referent of its corresponding descriptive term. So Putnam must now separate truth and 'ordinary' warrant, just as he had previously separated referent and stereotype. Hence the alterations in his theory prove to be a further refinement of the older version, rather than an incorporation of Dummett's actual point.

[67]Cf. M. Dummett, "Bringing About the Past" and "The Reality of the Past," both in Dummett, 1978; cf. further E. K. Specht, N. Erichsen, and K. Schuettauf, 1987.

[68]Cf. L. Wittgenstein, 1969, §§620 and 661–63.

[69]A different formulation of constructivism from Dummett's states that to understand p is to grasp the conditions for its *use* (which may or may not include assertion). We adopt this alternative, and perhaps quite generally preferable, formulation here.

tation is given by indicating the conditions of its truth; and since, for a realist, an interpretation is a hypothesis about what the author—or the text itself—in fact intends, its meaning consists precisely in the situation which obtains if it is true, to wit that the author or text in fact intended what the interpreter says it intended.) What are the use-conditions of interpretations? A literary critic is justified in claiming that a poem means this or that when the critic has construed (parsed, 'read') the text *according to the rules for reading poetry.*[70] Thus in the case of a literary critical interpretation the supporting grounds of the interpretation consist simply in that subset of the literary rules which the critic uses to construe the text. As we have said repeatedly, there is in literary-critical practice *de facto* no decisive appeal to extra-linguistic facts such as the author's intention. Hence liter-

---

[70]College textbooks used in introductory courses on the reading of poetry teach these rules and conventions, which are simultaneously the constitutive rules of poetry itself. See for example C. Brooks and R. P. Warren, 1976, or L. Perrine, 1982. A more concise statement of the major conventions of poetry is contained in chapter 8 of J. Culler, 1975. One such rule (that of 'organicity') stipulates, on the one hand, that every aspect of a poem contribute to the overall meaning; while at the same time it demands that interpretations be *global*, i.e., that they account in a unified manner for the presupposed organic unity of the text. Specht's criticism of Morwitz, for example, is that Morwitz simply ignores George's striking reference to "two poplars . . . [and] a pine in the meadow," thereby violating this rule (essay 4, pp. 156–57). This amounts to the charge that Morwitz *mis*uses the rules, and that thus his interpretation is *not warranted.* Such issues are seldom completely clear-cut. The crucial point, however, is that Specht's criticism proceeds from *another reading of the text*, i.e., another use of the rules to produce a different construal. Thus the two readings, though they differ, do not contradict one another, since each is rooted in a different construal. And, if constructivism is right, though construals may be more or less plausible (and some may even be absurd), *none* is true, none false, and therefore no one can contradict another. For the literary rules *manifestly* allow many readings. A construal which fails to conform with the rules is judged illicit or absurd, rather than false. This seems to be Gadamer's charge against Guardini in essay 2.

ary-critical interpretations have a status analogous to that of what linguists call 'readings' of sentences (as opposed to statements): in each case a bit of language (respectively the literary text and the sentence) is elucidated, and the elucidation appeals *not* to empirical features of the environment (e.g., the author's or speaker's intention), but to the linguistic rules governing the meaning of literary texts, on the one hand, or of words and phrases, on the other.[71]

At this point one similarity has ended between literary interpretations and more familiar constructivist examples (such as statements dealing with the past or with other minds). For in the case of literary interpretations we cannot say (as we can in the other cases) that 'the assertion of a particular interpretation might be fully justified *even though it later turns out to be false.*' The reason is, of course, that hermeneutical constructivists (Gadamer, Specht) deny the existence of any tribunal by appeal to which a literary interpretation could be shown to be true or false. Hence to the case of literary interpretation we cannot apply certain formulations of semantic constructivism, to wit those which say that one understands the meaning of a statement 'if one knows what justifies the assertion that the statement *is true.*'[72] Indeed the more familiar constructivist examples concerning the past and other minds have this about them, that in such cases a decision seems to be *imaginable.* This was the point of our remark above (pp. 59–60) that a more refined version of realism attempts to deal with such examples by treating them as ones in which a decision, though not accessible to *us*, is imaginable

[71]This analysis shows the substantial truth in Dilthey's version of the autonomy thesis. See above, p. 12. E. D. Hirsch, incidentally, notes the analogy between 'readings' and what we would call constructivistically construed interpretations, and, finding it intolerable uses it as an argument *in favor of* author-intentional criticism, arguing that only so will interpretations be decidable (see Hirsch, 1967, p. 225). This is to make philosophical hermeneutics the judge, and not the description or reconstruction, of hermeneutical practice.

[72]Cf. for example Dummett's formulation, in Dummett, 1979.

for an omniscient being to whom all of history is present and who sees into the hidden recesses of the mind. This version of realism relies upon the view that the contents of history and of other minds, though surely hidden from us, are nonetheless *there*. Dummett of course finds this kind of view unacceptable.

In any event, if hermeneutical constructivism's self-description is correct, we cannot explain it as the view that to understand an interpretation is to grasp the conditions which justify its assertion '*even if it should later turn out to be false*', for there is in principle no way to verify or falsify such interpretations, even for an omniscient being. That is one reason why we substituted 'use' for 'assertion' above. The case of literary-critical interpretations is semantically so interesting precisely because it removes what can be a lingering doubt about constructivism. The received arguments of Dummett and others (concerning other minds, the past, etc.) can seem to hinge on a *lack of information* which in principle could be overcome: a time-machine could take us back to the past, a divinity could verify or falsify statements about the inner lives of others; thus, one might persist in thinking, the truth-conditions of such statements are only inaccessible in practice (not in principle), and hence are indeed suited to be the meanings of the statements in question. Literary-critical interpretations, however, are eminently meaningful in the absence of *any* truth-conditions, available or imaginable. Hence such interpretations represent an especially strong proof that meaning is not generally to be equated with truth-conditions.

Let us summarize: our reconstruction of the recent German hermeneutics debate has concerned the question whether it makes sense to speak of *the* (unique) meaning of a literary text, the meaning which would be the goal of a scientifically conceived literary criticism. If we now follow Wittgenstein's suggestion[73] and replace the question "What *is* the meaning of a literary text?" with "How do we explain the

---

[73]L. Wittgenstein, 1958, p. 1.

meaning of a literary text?"[74] then it becomes immediately clear that the meaning of, say, a poem is explained by means of a literary-critical interpretation. (Gadamer might say that such texts have meaning only as part of a process of being read, i.e., interpreted.) It is precisely in the interpretive context that we speak of 'what a literary text means'. And it is our contention that a literary-critical interpretation (i.e., an explanation of the meaning of the literary text) in fact proceeds by appealing not to the author's (or text-) intention, but rather to what we have called 'the rules for reading poetry'. These are the conditions which justify the interpretation.

Of course even a justified interpretation cannot claim to be the one, true reading of the text. But precisely this notion that a proper interpretation *should* have this sort of uniqueness is the 'mental cramp' which the Wittgensteinian shift in questions is meant to loosen.

But now it seems that we have spoken of 'meaning' in two rather different senses: first, there is the meaning of the literary text, which is given by an interpretation, and second, there is the meaning of the interpretation itself, which is given by showing the (sub-)set of the literary rules which justify the interpreter's claim. And this much is true: the meanings in question are in fact given in different ways, hence one must say of them that they *are* different kinds of meaning; for literary texts (unlike interpretations) are of course *not asserted*. On the other hand, we have stressed that literary texts have their meaning *only* in being read, i.e., interpreted; and naturally there would be no literary interpretations if there were no literary texts. Hence we have here the interesting case in which what *prima facie* seem to be two language-games (that of writing poetry and that of criticizing it), each with its own kind of meaning, are so closely meshed that neither could subsist alone: hence there is but one game which contains two distinct kinds of usage.

Two questions remain to be answered. First, according to realist semantics the interpretation of texts is decidable by

[74]Cf. L. Wittgenstein, 1954, §§533–34.

appeal to the author's (or the text's) intention. But in fact in the practice of literary criticism the author's intention is treated as merely another interpretation and is often overruled; and the claim that the text-intention is there to be discovered is apparently just a relic, a wraith of the thesis of the author's intention. However, in rejecting realist semantics one still has to concede that it accords well with the *attitude* of the practicing literary critic, who after all wants to give the uniquely true interpretation. How is this 'realist' attitude of practicing critics to be reconciled with the constructivist reality of their craft?

The first step to reconciliation is to repair the misapprehension that in the absence of governing truth-conditions, interpretation must become totally arbitrary. In fact, constructivism *implies* that an interpretation must be well-grounded: a construal which does not proceed 'by the rules' is judged illicit or absurd, i.e., not a proper interpretation at all. Interpreting is a craft, an exacting one, and not a matter of free association and arbitrary fantasy. The 'realist error' is to see in the exacting standards of literary criticism the mark of decidability. The constructivist corrective consists in showing that an interpretation of textual meaning is constructed by the interpreter relying solely on one or another subset of the literary rules. In this task the critic will unavoidably be influenced by the prejudices of his or her time. Hence constructivism offers a semantical reconstruction of Gadamer's provocative thesis that everytime we understand, we understand *differently*.[75]

Finally, there is the question whether we can reasonably speak of the 'autonomy of the hermeneutical disciplines'. It is our view that Gadamer is substantially correct in his claim that what marks the humanities is their concern with meaning and hence, in the dialectic of *sich in der Sache verstehen*, with self-knowledge: all interpretation is guided by the reader's prejudices; positive prejudices make it possible to understand at all, and interpreters who proceed properly (i.e., with 'con-

[75]Gadamer, 1960/1975, p. 280/264.

sciousness of the history of influence') simultaneously gain understanding both of the text and of their own prejudices (self-knowledge). In the light of our semantical reconstruction this means that interpreters who become aware of themselves, of their own prejudices, understand this: that interpetations are undecidable.

Seen from the standpoint of constructivism, Gadamer challenges us to dissolve, again and again, a stubborn confusion, to wit the view that we could, through the use of 'method', somehow or other attain that omniscient viewpoint from which the *de facto* hidden truth or falsity of every undecided proposition is revealed. But this view is an illusion: the fact that some propositions cannot be decided, once and for all, does not mark a deficiency, but instead an opportunity for deeper self-knowledge. There is more than one kind of knowledge, and the kind which the humanisitic disciplines offer us comes first and foremost from their capacity to confront us, through eminent texts, with ourselves.

1
On the Circle of Understanding

Hans-Georg Gadamer

The hermeneutical rule that we must understand the whole from the individual and the individual from the whole stems from ancient rhetoric and was carried over by modern hermeneutics from the art of speaking to the art of understanding. There is in both cases a circular relationship. The anticipation of meaning, in which the whole is projected, is brought to explicit comprehension in that the parts, determined by the whole, determine this whole as well.

This is familiar to us from learning foreign languages. We learn that we can only try to understand the parts of a sentence in their linguistic meaning when we have parsed or construed the sentence. But the process of parsing is itself guided by an expectation of meaning arising from the preceding context. Of course this expectation must be corrected as the text requires. This means then that the expectation is transposed and that the text is consolidated into a unified meaning under another expectation. Thus the movement of understanding always runs from whole to part and back to whole. The task is to expand in concentric circles the unity of the understood meaning. Harmonizing all the particulars with the whole is at each stage the criterion of correct understanding. Its absence means the failure to understand.

Schleiermacher differentiated this hermeneutical circle both according to its subjective, and according to its objective, sides. Just as the individual word belongs to the context of the sentence, so too the individual text belongs to the context of an author's works, and these to the whole of the literary genre in question or the whole of literature itself. On the other side, however, the same text belongs, as manifestation of a creative moment, to the whole of its author's inner life. Understanding can be completed only in such a whole composed of objective and subjective parts. With reference to this theory Dilthey then speaks of "structure" and of "centering in a middle-point," from which the comprehension of the whole follows. He thereby transposes to the historical world an age-old rule of all interpretation: that one must understand a text in its own terms.

The question arises, however, whether in this manner the circular movement of understanding is properly understood. We can indeed leave completely aside what Schleiermacher set forth as subjective interpretation. When we try to understand a text, we do not place ourselves in the author's inner state; rather, if one wants to speak of 'placing oneself', we place ourselves in his point of view. But this means nothing else than that we try to let stand the claim to correctness of what the other person says. We will even, if we want to understand, attempt to strengthen his arguments. If it works this way even in conversation, how much more so in the understanding of what is written, where we move in a dimension of meaningfulness which is understandable in itself and as such motivates no recourse to the subjectivity of the other person. It is the task of hermeneutics to illuminate this miracle of understanding, which is not a mysterious communication of souls, but rather a participation in shared meaning.

But the objective side of this circle, as Schleiermacher describes it, is equally wide of the mark. The goal of all communication and all understanding is agreement in the matter at hand. Thus from time immemorial hermeneutics has had as its task to restore lagging or interrupted agreement. This can be confirmed by the history of hermeneutics, if one thinks for example of Augustine, when the issue was to mediate the Old Testament and the Christian Gospel; or of early Protestantism, which faced the same problem; or finally of the Age of Enlightenment, in which, if the "complete understanding" of a text was meant to be reached only by way of historical interpretation, this amounted in practice to a renunciation of agreement. There is now something qualitatively new when Romanticism and Schleiermacher, in creating a historical consciousness with universal scope, no longer acknowledge the binding form of the tradition from which they come and in which they stand as the firm basis for all hermeneutical labors. One of Schleiermacher's immediate predecessors, the philologist Friedrich Ast, still had a decidedly content-oriented understanding of the task of hermeneutics when he demanded that it establish agreement between antiquity and Christianity, between a newly appreciated, true antiquity and the Christian tradition. Compared with the Enlightenment this is, to be sure, something new in that it is no longer a matter of mediating between the authority of tradition and natural reason but rather of mediating two elements of the tradition which, having both been brought to awareness by the Enlightenment, set the task of their own reconciliation.

Indeed it seems to me that a doctrine like this of the unity of antiquity and Christianity latches onto an essential aspect of the hermeneutical phenomenon, one which Schleiermacher and his successors wrongly surrendered. Ast's speculative energy kept him here from looking for mere pastness, as opposed to the truth of the present, in history. In front of this backdrop the hermeneutics derived from Schleiermacher seems a shallowing out into methodology.

This applies even more when one views that hermeneutics in the light of the formulation of the question developed by Heidegger. That is to say, from the vantage point of Heidegger's existential analysis the circular structure of understanding regains its content-oriented meaning. He writes: "The circle must not be denigrated to a vicious, or even to a tolerated, circle. In it lies hidden the positive potentiality of the most original knowledge, which of course is only genuinely grasped if the interpretation has understood that its first, permanent, and final task remains that of not accepting from flashes of inspiration and popular notions a pretence of its own fore-having, fore-sight, and fore-conception, but rather to work these out of the subject matter itself and thereby to secure the topic under study]"[1]

What Heidegger is saying here is not, in the first instance, a demand issued to the practice of understanding, rather it describes the form in which the interpretation which produces understanding is accomplished. Heidegger's hermeneutical reflection has its point not so much in proving the existence of this circle as in showing its ontologically positive meaning. His description will be evident as such to any interpreter who knows what he is doing.[2] All correct interpretation has to screen itself against arbitrary whims and the narrowness of imperceptible habits of thinking, training its sights "on the objects themselves" (which for philologists are meaningful texts which for their part again treat of objects).

To let oneself be determined in this way by the objects is obviously no one-time "scout's honor" resolution, but really "the first, permanent, and final task." For it is a question of fixing one's gaze on the object through all the diversions with which the interpreter constantly assails himself along the way. Whoever wants to understand a text, is always carrying out a projection. From the moment a first meaning becomes apparent in the text he projects a meaning of the whole. On the other hand it is only because one from the start reads the text with certain expectations of a definite meaning that an initial meaning becomes apparent. It is in working out this sort of projection—which of course is constantly being revised in the light of what emerges with deeper penetration into the meaning—that the understanding of what is there consists.

This description is of course a crude abbreviation: that every revision of the projection has the potentiality of itself projecting a new design; that rival projections can bring forward one another to be worked through side by side until the

---

[1]Heidegger, 1927/1962, p. 153/195. [The translation given here is our own—Eds.]

[2]Cf., for example, E. Staiger's concordant description in Staiger, 1955, p. 11 ff.

unity of the meaning determines itself more clearly; that interpretation begins with fore-concepts that are replaced by more suitable concepts: exactly this constant re-designing, constitutive of the back-and-forth of meaning in understanding and interpreting, is the process which Heidegger describes. Anyone who tries to understand is exposed to the diversions of pre-opinions which fail to prove their worth when faced with the objects. Thus the constant task of understanding is to work out the proper, objectively appropriate projections, i.e., to hazard anticipations which are supposed to be confirmed only 'by application to the objects.' Here there is no other 'objectivity' than working out that pre-opinion which meets the test. It makes good sense for the interpreter, animated by his ready pre-opinion, not to tackle the 'text' straight off, but rather to test the living pre-opinion in himself for its legitimacy, i.e., for its provenance and validity.

We must think of this basic demand as the radicalization of a device which we in truth always apply. Far from it being the case that whoever listens to someone else or approaches a literary text must bring along no pre-opinion about the content and must forget all his own opinions, it is rather the case that openness for the opinion of the other or of the text will always include setting it in relation to the whole of one's own opinions or setting oneself to it. Put differently, opinions are indeed a changeable variety of possibilities, but within this variety of what people can think, i.e., of what a reader can find sensible and thus can expect, not everything is possible; and whoever 'hears past' what the other is really saying will not in the end be able to fit it into his own manifold expectation of meaning. So here too there is a standard. The hermeneutical task turns on its own into a question about the objects of discussion and is determined by this from the start. In this way the hermeneutical enterprise acquires a firm footing. Whoever wants to understand will not rely on the fortuitousness of his own pre-opinions, so as to 'hear past' the text's opinion as consistently and stubbornly as possible—until it becomes deafening and topples the would-be understanding. Rather, the person who wants to understand a text is ready to be told something by it. So a hermeneutically trained mind must from the start be open to the otherness of the text. But such openness presupposes neither "neutrality" about the objects of study nor indeed self-obliteration, but rather includes the identifiable appropriation of one's own pre-opinions and prejudices. One has to be aware of one's own bias, so that the text presents itself in its otherness and in this manner has the chance to play off its truth in the matter at hand against the interpreter's pre-opinion.

Heidegger gave a perfectly correct phenomenological description when he uncovered the pre-structure of understanding in the alleged 'reading' of 'what's right there.' He also gave an example to show that a task follows from this. In *Being and Time* he concretizes, in treating the question of being, his general statement about the hermeneutical problem.[3] To explicate the hermeneutical situation of the question of being about fore-having, fore-sight, and fore-conception he critically tested the question which he directed at metaphysics on essential turning points in the history of metaphysics. In this way he did what historical-hermeneutical consciousness demands in every case. An understanding guided by methodical awareness will have to take pains not simply to ratify its own anticipation, but rather to make it conscious so as to control it and thereby to attain from the objects of study themselves the correct understanding. This is what Heidegger means when he demands that in working out fore-having, fore-sight, and fore-conception we "secure" the topic of research out of the subject matter itself.

In Heidegger's analysis the hermeneutical circle thus gains a quite new meaning. In the theory up to his time the circular structure of understanding was confined within the framework of a formal relation between individual and whole, or within its subjective reflection, the prescient anticipation of the whole and its subsequent explication in the individual parts. So according to this view the circular movement ran

---

[3]Heidegger, 1927/1962, pp. 312 ff./360 ff.

back and forth in the text and was consummated when the text itself was completely understood. The theory of understanding reached its peak in a divinatory act of putting oneself into the author and dissolving from this vantage point all the alien and surprising aspects of the text. Against this Heidegger recognizes that the understanding of the text remains permanently determined by the anticipatory movement of the pre-understanding. What Heidegger describes in this way is nothing other than the task of concretizing the historical consciousness. This requires one to be aware of one's own pre-opinions and prejudices, and to permeate the act of understanding with historical awareness so that the comprehension of the historically different and the requisite application of historical methods do not merely reckon out what one has first put in.

Our understanding of the content-relevant sense of the whole-part circle at the base of all understanding must, however, as I believe, be expanded to accomodate a further feature, which I would like to call "the anticipation of perfection." In this way a presupposition is formulated which guides all understanding. It says that one can only understand that which represents a perfect unity of meaning. For example, we make this presupposition of perfection whenever we read a text. We only call this presupposition into question if it proves irredeemable, i.e., the text does not become comprehensible; perhaps we begin to have doubts about the authenticity of the text and set out to confirm it. We can here leave aside the rules which we follow in such text-critical considerations, since what matters is that here too we cannot detach our right to apply them from our grasp of the text's content.

The anticipation of perfection which guides all our understanding thus turns out to be one determined in each case by content. We presuppose not only an immanent unity of meaning, which gives the reader guidance, but the reader's comprehension is also constantly guided by transcendent expectations of meaning which arise from the relationship to the truth of what is meant. Just as the addressee of a letter understands the news he receives and, to begin with, sees things with the eyes of the letter-writer, i.e., takes what the writer says to be true—instead of, say, trying to understand the writer's opinion as such—so we too understand the texts which are handed down on the basis of expectations of meaning drawn from our own relationship to the issues under discussion. And just as we believe the reports of a correspondent because he was there or in some other way knows better, so too we are basically open to the possibility that the text which has come down to us knows better than our own pre-opinion wants to admit. It is only the failure of the attempt to admit what is said as true that leads to the endeavor to "understand"—psychologically or historically—the text as the opinion of another.[4] Thus the prejudice of perfection comprises not only that a text is supposed to express its opinion completely, but also that what it says is the complete truth. To understand means primarily to understand [oneself in] the subject matter,[5] and only secondarily to detach and understand the opinion of the other as such. The first of all hermeneutical conditions consequently remains understanding of the subject matter, i.e., having to do with the same object. From it is determined what can be worked out as a unified meaning and thus the application of the anticipation of perfection. In this way the meaning of belonging, i.e., the moment of tradition in historical-hermeneutical behavior, is fulfilled through the commonality of basic and supporting prejudices. Hermeneutics must proceed from the assumption that whoever wants to understand has a bond with the subject matter that is articulated in what is handed down, and is, or becomes, connected with the tradition out of which what is handed down speaks. On the other hand the hermeneutical consciousness knows that it cannot be connected with this subject matter in the manner of an un-

---

[4]In a lecture on the aesthetic judgment at a congress in Venice [Gadamer, 1958] I set out to show that the aesthetic judgment, like the historical variety, also has secondary character and confirms the "anticipation of perfection."

[5][For an explanation of our translation of the phrase *sich in der Sache verstehen*, see our Introduction, p. 31, note 44—Eds.]

questioned implicit accord such as obtains in the case of the unbroken continuity of a tradition. There really is a polarity of familiarity and strangeness on which the task of hermeneutics is based, although this is not to be understood psychologically with Schleiermacher as the span concealing the secret of an individuality; but rather truly hermeneutically, i.e., with respect to what is said: the language with which what is handed down speaks to us, the saying which it says to us. The position between strangeness and familiarity which what is handed down has for us is thus the Between between historically meant, distanced objectivism and belonging to a tradition. In this Between is the true place of hermeneutics.

It follows from this in-between position, in which it has its foothold, that its center is what remained at the edge of hermeneutics up to now: temporal distance and the meaning it has for understanding. Time is not primarily an abyss to be bridged because it divides and holds apart, it is rather in truth the supporting ground of the event in which present understanding has its roots. Thus temporal distance is not something to be overcome. That was rather the naive presupposition of historicism, that one imagines oneself into the spirit of the times, that one thinks in their concepts and ideas and not in one's own, and in this manner forges forward to historical objectivity.

It is in truth a matter of recognizing the distance of time as a positive and productive possibility for understanding. It is filled up by the continuity of custom and tradition, in the light of which all of what is handed down reveals itself to us. Here it is not too much to speak of a genuine productivity of the event. Everyone knows the peculiar powerlessness of our judgment wherever temporal distance has not entrusted us with sure criteria. Thus for the academic consciousness judgment about contemporary art is desperately insecure. There are obviously uncontrollable prejudices with which we approach such creations and which are capable of bestowing on them an excess of resonance which fails to conform with the true content and the true meaning of those works. Not until all such topical connections die off can their true shape become visible, thereby allowing an understanding of what they say which can make a binding claim to universality. Filtering out the true meaning contained in a text or an artistic creation is, incidentally, itself an unending process. The temporal distance which accomplishes this filtering is engaged in a constant movement and enlargement, and this is the productive side which it possesses for understanding. It lets prejudices which catch only a part of the work die off, while letting those emerge which make possible a true understanding.

Nothing but this temporal distance is capable of solving the actual critical task of hermeneutics, that of separating true from false prejudices. The hermeneutically trained consciousness will therefore include a historical consciousness. It will have to make conscious the prejudices guiding understanding so that what is handed down, as a different opinion, stands out and makes itself seen. To let a prejudice stand out as such obviously requires a suspension of its validity; for, as long as a prejudice is influencing us, we do not know and consider it as a judgment. To bring, as it were, a prejudice to my own attention cannot succeed as long as this prejudice is constantly and inconspicuously in play, but rather only when it is, so to speak, stirred up. What is capable of this sort of stirring up is the encounter with what is handed down. For whatever entices us to understand has first to have made itself prominent in its otherness. The first thing with which understanding begins is that something speaks to us. That is the supreme hermeneutical requirement. We now see what this demand involves: a basic suspension of one's own prejudices. But all suspension of judgments—consequently and above all the suspension of prejudices—has in logical terms the structure of a question.

The essence of a question is to open up possibilities and keep them open. If a prejudice is called into question—in the face of what someone else or a text says to us—it does not as a result mean that it simply gets set aside, while in its place the other person or other thing immediately makes itself felt. It is rather the naiveté of historical objectivism to assume such a turning away from oneself. The truth is that one's own prejudice only really gets involved in the game by becoming itself at stake in the game. Only by playing out its role can it become so teamed up with the other that it too [the other] can play out its role.

The naiveté of so-called historicism consists in its shunning such reflection, and—in trusting in the methodology of its procedure—forgetting its own historicity. Here an appeal must be made from a poorly understood mode of historical thinking to one to be understood more adequately. A truly historical way of thinking has also to keep in mind its own historicity. Only then will it give up pursuing the phantom of a historical object, the topic of linearly advancing research, learning instead to recognize in the object the Other of its Own, therewith bringing to recognition the One and the Other. The true historical object is not an object, but rather the unity of this One and Other, a relationship in which the reality of history consists just as much as the reality of historical understanding. A hermeneutics equal to its object would have to exhibit this essential reality of history in understanding itself. I name what is contained in this requirement "the history of influence" (*Wirkungsgeschichte*).[6] Understanding is a process in the history of influence, and it could be proven that it is in the linguisticality belonging to all understanding that the hermeneutical event makes its path.

---

[6][For an explanation of our translation of *Wirkungsgeschichte* (and the related term, *wirkungsgeschichtliches Bewußtsein* see our Introduction, p. 33, n. 47—Eds.]

2

Mythopoetic Inversion in Rilke's *Duino Elegies*

HANS-GEORG GADAMER

All interpretation is one-sided. It aims at a target, an aspect which can lay no claim to uniqueness. This is especially the case with poetry, which can be interpreted from very different points of view: the interpreter can proceed from the history of the genre by locating the work in question in a tradition of exemplars of the same literary genre; he can also proceed from the history of motifs by pursuing the adoption and modification of certain received themes; or he can elaborate the rhetorical-poetic devices and their connection to the whole of a 'structure', etc. But he can also take on the original hermeneutical task of explaining what is unintelligible. And in this process, further, he can proceed 'occasionally' (as did Protestant New Testament hermeneutics and philology up until the late eighteenth century), seeking to eliminate—by

---

This essay, first presented in Mainz at a presemester theology seminar (October 1966), owes its origin to my disappointment over the wasted exertions in Jakob Steiner's industrious commentary (Steiner, 1962). Only with difficulty have I withstood the temptation to correct, where I could, the detailed individual explanations which are there amassed. The present essay coincides with much that I already wrote twelve years ago in my critique of Guardini (Guardini, 1953, Gadamer, 1954–55, 1967b). Nonetheless, the theoretical interest in the hermeneutical principle seemed to me to demand more explicit treatment as well as testing on an example.

means of analysis of the context, the drawing of parallels, etc.—the individual difficulties to which unintelligible passages give rise; or he will start from the unity of what is said and seek to interpret what the poem wants to say, this latter chiefly in the case of poems which possess a high level of reflection and are therefore regarded on the whole as obscure and difficult to understand.

Rilke's *Duino Elegies* belong to this kind of poetry and require, in the first instance, an interpretation of this kind, which in the event has been copiously bestowed on them. First came the theologians, then the philosophers and a lot of ideologically committed authors. All of them pursued the endeavor of translating what the poetry says into the prose of their thoughts and the binding truth of their concepts. About the text and its precise rendering there was for the most part not a lot said. To be sure no interpretation of poetry is imaginable (or at least ought not to be) without the interpreter's commitment. But at the same time it represents a constant seduction to read and hear out of the text that which most willingly complies with one's own preconceptions, even if this results in the violation of the canon of understanding given by the coherence of the sense of the whole.

Quite recently literary scholarship has begun to make the *Elegies* its object of study and to look precisely at the text, which thereupon, however, tends to break up into words. Thus Jakob Steiner's industriously and conscientiously elaborated commentary is more a commentary on the words, one which in particular makes very extravagant use of parallels. But it is a delicate problem what contributions, if any, parallels are able to make to the interpretation of poetry. To be sure, they always have a certain approximate value for ascertaining linguistic usage, interpreting individual motifs, and so on. However, if even in other philological cases it is very difficult and rare to find parallels which are really correct, it is far worse in the case of the interpretation of poetry, in that even those parallels which are correct bring with them the danger of clashing with the resonance awakened by the unity of poetic discourse.

If today—in an epoch that is carried upward on the wave of a new enlightenment, leaving ever narrower room for poetic statement, so that it decidedly emphasizes the pathos of matter-of-factness, understatement, epigrammatic allusion, and reportorial sidelight—one returns to Rilke (who in the 1930s and early 1940s was the poet capable, by the extreme mannerism of his linguistic attitude, of most deeply sustaining the consciousness of the time, especially the consciousness resistant to 'political coordination' [*Gleichschaltung*]), an awareness of another sort is required. Certainly "to get a grip on what grasps us" (E. Staiger) is a genuine need which we experience with respect to all poetry, and in comparison to the committed translations of days gone by this need has taken on a different shape. Not in the sense of literary-scholarly analysis and comment, nor in the sense of those pre-committed applications, but rather in this way: Rilke's poetic language, which still has the indisputable presence of great poetry, calls out—across all the distance of an immensely altered life-feeling—for a clarification of the horizon which encloses it. The time seems finally to have come for attaining, by means of an explicit unfolding of the hermeneutic horizon, the level of reflection on which Rilke's poetry moves, and for leaving behind what has heretofore been the concern of the interpreters, the unmediated pronouncement of theological or philosophical truth.[1]

Whoever wants to attain the level of reflection on which the *Duino Elegies* are at home must first of all free himself from all theological and pseudo-religious anticipations,[2] as if via the discrete detour of the angel, God were being spoken of in these poems. Instead, the subject of the *Elegies* can be deter-

---

[1]As the example of Jakob Steiner shows, the instructions which I tried to give twelve years ago in my Guardini-criticism [Gadamer, 1954–55], have not at all been heeded. [The reader might compare that review-discussion, and especially its first footnote, with this present essay.—Eds.]

[2][Or, more literally, 'fore-conceptions'. Cf. our Introduction, pp. 18–19—Eds.].

mined in a very simple, hermeneutically recommended way, and it is astonishing that the Rilke literature has heretofore not trod this path. I mean the fact that, at the very time the *Elegies*, whose genesis stretched out over a decade, were ordered into a cycle and prepared for publication by the poet, the then fifth elegy was exchanged for one newly composed. We read the poem which had to make way for the new elegy under the title "Antistrophes."[3]

That it had to make way for the new poem, which we know as the "Elegy of the (Itinerant) Acrobats," is easily accounted for. Today's fifth elegy forms a far better stylistic unit with the other nine: the same free-wheeling verse formation, the same comprehensive sense-expression, the same artistically indirect world of images. By contrast the "Antistrophes" tackle their theme directly, though also artistically, and quite exclude themselves formally, as well, by virtue of their almost strophically effective response-form. But that makes it all the more significant that this poem was once able to take the position of the fifth among these ten elegies. Its direct, uncoded statement therewith takes on a genuinely binding character for the whole. It declares a central theme of the elegies:

> "O that you women go about
> here among us
> sorrowfully, no more spared than we
> and nonetheless able
> to bless as do the Blessed."

It is the theme which in the *Sonnets to Orpheus* goes:

> "Not learned is love."

The fifth elegy also ends in this theme, when it turns the make-believe construction of the acrobatic troupe toward the image of longing which would represent the truly happy union of the lovers.

---

[3][Reprinted, with English translation by Michael Hamburger, in Rilke, 1981.]

Like all elegies Rilke's *Duino Elegies* are laments. What is lamented is the unattainability of true happiness for lovers, or rather: the incapacity of lovers, and especially the man in love, to love in such a way that true fulfillment would become possible. Therewith, however, the theme of the elegies is broadened to something more general. The issue is the powerlessness of the human heart, its failure before the task of surrendering itself completely to its feeling. The "Antistrophes" are able to lament over the fact that a woman in love is better at this than a man. Similarly the *Elegies* begin with the "eternal" lovers, those who have been abandoned but still go on loving. The area, however, which it paces off covers more ground. Linked with the experience of love is the experience of death, both obviously experiences whose demands are so great that the human heart cannot but become aware of its failure. It is in particular those who die young who make the mourner aware of the powerlessness of his heart. What he is unable to manage, evidently, is to accept it as it is, mourning and lamenting, but without lapsing into accusations against the cruelty of a fate such as the death of children and youths: what is called for is to remove "the appearance of injustice."[4]

In roughly this manner we can describe the initial experience and the whole compass of that with which the *Elegies* deal. We must start from this fore-understanding—forced upon us by the poetry itself—of what is spoken of, if we want to understand how it is spoken of, i.e., we have to attain that horizon of understanding and interpretation within which the poetic statement can be realized with precision.

At the forefront stands the question of what the angel of the *Elegies* means. To answer this question we have no need of the self-interpretation which Rilke gave and which in any event led him much too far into spiritualistic dogmatics. The

---

[4]Rilke, 1939, I, lines 66–67. [Note that we have quite generally used our own, very literal translations, though we consulted the Leishman-Spender version in each instance—Eds.]

angel is, to be sure, a superhuman being and is appealed to as a being infinitely exceeding us in the capacity to feel, but in no way does he appear as a messenger or representative of God and he bears witness to no transcendence, in the religious sense, at all. When Rilke at one point calls him the guarantor of the invisible, this characterization too is anything but theological. The invisible is that which cannot be seen or touched but which is nonetheless real. In the human heart it is the reality of its feeling, which lays claim to such indisputable certainty without being able to prove itself. This reality must thus assert itself against the utilitarian skepticism of a massive realism which despises the luxury of the emotions. When now the angel confirms the insistence on the reality of what we feel, this means that the conditionality and incompleteness of our emotions, which could arouse doubt about their reality, is, with the figure of the angel, lifted above all question. His feeling is unconditioned and unambiguous to an extent which the human heart is capable of feeling only at rare moments.

Thus it is one of the highest possibilities of the human heart itself which is called upon as angel—a possibility before which it fails, which it cannot manage, because many things condition human beings, making them incapable of unequivocality and unrestricted surrender to their feelings. This is confirmed by the poetic situations in which, in the *Elegies*, we and the angel are spoken of: "I would grow faint from his stronger existence,"[5] "beating beyond its wont, our own heart would strike us dead,"[6] "we, when we feel, vanish into the air,"[7] the angel of the fourth elegy, who "plays over and above us";[8] and then again and again the angel to whom something is shown: the strenuous smile of the child-acrobat, the hardship of the acrobats' fate, but also the great works of human art, into

[5]*Duino Elegies*, I, lines 3–4.
[6]Ibid., II, lines 8–9.
[7]Ibid., II, line 18.
[8]Ibid., IV, lines 61–62.

which feeling has entered, and—on this side of all lofty emotions—the world of things, before which the human heart is always wont to fail by heedlessly looking past it. Again and again it is the power and powerlessness of human feeling which gives occasion for thinking of the angel as one whose feeling is not limited by the feeling of something else, but instead so fills him that his emotion is completely identical with him. An emotion which does not evaporate but which rather stands in itself is what Rilke calls 'angel', because such feeling surpasses human beings. Women, as they are addressed in the first of the "Antistrophes," are in Rilke's eyes a little closer to the angel.

There is no doubt that Rilke was completely unfamiliar with the medieval Christian theology of angels. As is well known, he even explicitly repudiated the connection with the angel-conception of Christianity. All the same there is in the idea 'angel' an ontological problem which apparently comes through everywhere: medieval thought was very exercised over the idea that angels are identical with their task and thus cannot possess 'time' in the sense of human temporal consciousness, neither time nor eternity.[9] Nor is the angel of the *Elegies* either a human or a divine apparition—he does not appear at all unless the human heart musters up the unequivocality which could summon him. ("Against such a strong current you can make no headway.") The call of the poetic speaker to the angel is not a call which would summon anyone. It is more nearly the invocation of, and the call to, a witness who is supposed to confirm that which one already knows. What one knows oneself, that of which one is so aware and has such inner certainty that it is inseparable from oneself: it is this which here (with Rilke) is called feeling and emotion. Opinion and appearance can alter, can be given up, disappear, etc.; emotion, the most fleeting of all—wanting to hold onto which, even *wanting* this is senseless—retains an unambiguous reality, in which there is nothing at all except itself, and which, as we say, completely captivates and fills us.

[9]Cf. Thomas Aquinas, *De Instantibus* (in Baeumker, 1898, pp. 160ff).

But what does it mean when this limit concept of our own being is called upon as an angel, i.e., as an agent? At this point we must bring to bear a hermeneutical reflection on the question of how any poetic discourse is understood. All poetic discourse is myth, that is, it certifies itself through nothing more than its being said. It tells a story, or speaks of deeds and events, and yet gains credence—but gain it it does—only to the extent that we ourselves are the ones who encounter ourselves in these actions and sufferings of gods and heroes. That is why, right down to the present, the mythical world of the ancients stimulates poets ever anew to revitalize it for the purpose of contemporary self-confrontation. Often in this process there is the most sophisticated awareness, inasmuch as poets realize that their own poetic ancestors are also present in the reader. Quite generally, the horizon of understanding into which the poet speaks is here reliably prepared.

Of course even then it does not mean that the ancient myth still contains a religious truth, and nonetheless it remains comprehensible, and this in a way which can of course only be conceptualized through the interpretation of successful poetic revitalizations. When—decades ago—Walter F. Otto was able to talk of the Homeric gods with the softly enraptured tone of an initiate, so that his listeners understood something, i.e., not only took note of religious curiosities but gained access to these gods out of human experiences, it was Homer who carried him (and when he undertook, not without profundity and subtlety, to unlock Dionysus, he did not advance beyond Nietzsche, because he lacked the revitalizing poetry).[10] In all such cases the principle of understanding is founded on an inversion: what presents itself as the action and suffering of others is understood as one's own suffering experience. The concept of 'demythologizing', so much debated in contemporary theology, also implies the principle of this inversion to the extent that the circle of meaning of the New

[10]Walter F. Otto, 1929 and 1933.

Testament religious proclamation is bounded by this invertibility into a human understanding of faith.[11]

One has to reassure oneself about this hermeneutical presupposition in order to grasp Rilke's special poetic mode of operation. Here it is no longer a question of the mythic tradition of antiquity (and its Christian permeation, which enabled an age as recent as the Baroque to create allegorically rich poetry) being carried on, not even in the form of a conscious revitalization, as was the case with, say, Hölderlin's later poetic works. Here we no longer have a mythical world, but what remains is the principle of poetic inversion. With Rilke it becomes 'mythopoetic' inversion: in the poetic saying the world of our own heart is set over against us as a mythical world, i.e., a world of active beings. That which surpasses the range of human feeling appears as an angel, the shock at the death of a young man appears as the dead young man, the lament which fills the human heart and follows the dead man appears as a being whom the dead young man follows: in short, it is the entire experiential dimension of the human heart which is poetically released into the autonomy of free individual being. What guides Rilke is the self-forgetfulness of mythic consciousness. By means of his highly manneristic art he succeeds in elevating, in a mythless present, the experiential world of the human heart to the level of the mythic-poetic.

The hermeneutical consequence is clear: the mythological phenomenon requires for its part a kind of hermeneutical inversion. One must retranslate the poetic statement. The methodological difficulty here, however, consists in the fact that what is to be retranslated is itself already something retranslated. Whereas in other cases the great mythical tradition is so to speak illuminated in a new poetic revitalization, fading off from this light into the inscrutable, the mythic real-

[11]R. Bultmann, however, defines 'myth' and 'mythic worldview' precisely as the opposite of the kerygma which is 'understood' in faith. But this involves a questionable dependence on the worldview of 'science', one which cannot limit the hermeneutical principle.

ity which unexpectedly shows up in Rilke's poetic discourse has each time the precise contours of a mere mirroring of some immanent experience. To reflect and retranslate these experiences as legible writing into our understanding cannot be done in the manner, say, in which a retranslation into conceptual prose regularly accompanies poetic understanding in times of fixed allegorical literary forms. Here we encounter no internally harmonious world of mythic figures, no expressly prepared comparisons, the unfolding of which for our contemporary understanding would be the hermeneutical task. Rather it is a sudden and unexpected evocation of harmony from which an apparently almost hermetic poetic structure spreads into our understanding. A certain amount of disharmony always remains in such understanding. But it is precisely the disharmony in the evocation of such harmonies which makes the poetic margins be moved.

In what follows the concrete application of the principle of mythopoetic inversion shall be presented using two elegies as examples. Let us begin with the fourth of the *Elegies*. Right away its opening offers the opportunity to try out our principle. The invocation "O trees of life" (line 1) means us. It is incorrect to read the second line with emphasis on "we." The stress lies on not being single-minded. We are not single-minded because we do not know when our winter is, like the tree of life (*arbor vitae*), which is evergreen. But that is only suggested, for the 'trees of life' are of course not *arbores vitae*. The splendid stroke of the opening line consists rather in the unmistakable self-address: the discourse—a lament—is about us. We are not like the migratory birds, who know their time, nor like the lions, who are in such unity with their royal gait that powerlessness, i.e., wanting something which one cannot achieve, does not touch them.

With these counterimages of unity the disunity and violence of all human behavior becomes lamentably apparent, and from our preparatory fore-understanding it is clear that it is above all lovers who here represent human behavior. The halfheartedness of our soul and the narrowness with which it enters into its feelings (so that we know the contour of our feeling not at all) cause us again and again to fall back from our devotion. The poet goes so far as to label as 'enmity' this irresistible insistence-on-ourselves, which narrows the devotion to others. Genuine devotion is wrested from its contrary, precisely this insistence-on-oneself, just "for the sketch of a moment" (line 14). That means: this insistence-on-oneself is as constant in us and spread out in all directions as the background against which a sketch stands out. "They are very plain with us" (lines 16–17)—the explainers have asked who is meant with "they." It is a simple case of mythopoetic inversion; it is we who are so plain with one another, in that we prepare the moments of genuine harmony with so much resistance, 'hearing past' one another, and insistence-on-ourselves that it is as if we did it intentionally, so that the devotion should be noticed for what it is. Of course "they" does not mean "we," but we are meant, as we are unable to do otherwise than as it comes to pass with us, as if we were not ourselves at all.

Just this experience of 'its coming to pass with us' forms the basis of the metaphorical character of everything which follows, the idea of sitting before one's own heart as before a stage, in timid expectation of what will be performed there, as if we were not ourselves at all. The timidity with which we anticipate the entrance on stage rests on the fact that we know we can never become completely one with the feeling which fills us, cannot—unlike the angel—hold on to being one with our feeling, this tumult of emotion, i.e., of the ever-increasing fullness of feeling. That is why the scenery on this stage of the heart is always departure. What is thereby meant is not the love-experiences coming to an end, but rather the prior knowledge that we are never equal to the task of being one with our feeling. That takes the form, in mythopoetic inversion, of the dancer's entrance, he who does his fake performance on a stage which wavers like scenery. The garden which promises to bring us its blossoms is fake, the unity of person and dance is only a pretense. One does not forget the dancer's private life, the life of a burgher, one who exerts himself when he plays his role and lets himself go when he gets home. In this manner the dancer represents the halfness, i.e., the strainedness, deliberateness of human feeling.

And the poet nonetheless sits in front of the stage of his own heart and awaits the complete, unbroken entrance of a true feeling. In this expectation of his heart, which ever expects genuine love, devotion obliterating all else, he lets nothing lead him astray. He summons witnesses—above all his father—to say that, in front of the stage of his own heart, it makes sense to expect true and entire feeling. Once again mythic inversion helps us to understand exactly. It is said of the father, who is long dead, that he has the equanimity of the dead—and he surrenders this equanimity for us. One understands that, inversely, the dead man is there for us in this manner: we have learned to get over the loss of him with equanimity. However this equanimity gets destroyed in certain life-situations. There are singular moments in life when the 'fore-I', the father, for a moment steps out of his imperturbable concealment. One thinks of him at those points at which one has to make serious decisions. And when at the end the angel has to come to pull the wires of the puppet-figures, this too is the description of a truth of self-understanding, to wit that there are experiences and decisions of our heart in which there is no more arbitrariness, no free choice, no more split at all between wanting this and wanting that, no more duality in one's heart. Then it really is as though it were a being far surpassing us that has taken us over entirely.

As proof that it is at all possible to stand in such unity with oneself and one's own feelings the poet offers in the sequel two witnesses: those who are dying and the child. The dying person, who has already closed accounts with himself, sees with undimmed clarity that everything around him is pretense. One thinks of Tolstoy's "Death of Ivan Ilitch": the visits of relatives and colleagues, the fake cheerfulness and the cramped appearance of confidence—the dying man follows, with an almost compassionate look, the spurious efforts of the living to conceal from him the fact that he must die. To that extent he is already more at one with himself.

And then the child. This witness of proper at-oneness with

oneself remains present right to the end of the poem. The child knows a complete involvement with the moment, indeed even his toy retains something of the same unconditionedness. For to the child the toy is at one moment everything, and at the next moment nothing. The way in which no continuity is claimed here shows what constitutes the existence of the child. Full presence, complete lack of past and future. Thus the totality of feeling is represented in the child, undivided agreement with itself.

This continues even to the extreme exaction of death. There is a chain of rhetorical questions: Who will show . . . , who . . . , who . . . ,(lines 76 ff.) which explicate the indescribable. For no one is capable of this task. It is so indescribable the way a child can stand there, entirely one with its own present being, an unattainable example of undivided and concentrated attention. The child too has its fate (it is placed in its constellation, lines 76–77), but it has in this the standard of distance. None of what happens to it is of the sort for it to dwell on, with a sense of resentment or loss or longing; instead it is "content (*vergnügt*) with what is lasting,"— a marvellous coinage of the word '*vergnügt*', in which the sufficient (*Genügende*) and the cheerful (*Vergnügte*) have become a unity. The child is not dependent on what happens to it: if one of its toys breaks, a game is destroyed, it gets called away or has some other sort of distress, how indeed does the child manage to pass so easily from the most extreme sorrow to the happiest smiles, and whence does it have this distance toward everything which happens to it?

This grand example of the child has its last trial and actual crucial test in the dying child. The manner in which the child is able to leave not only its toy, but everything in life to which it is attached extends all the way to the point at which the child leaves life itself when it dies. A child that has to die is like when rye bread becomes hard (lines 78–79), so natural and uninterrupted is the process. (There may also be an element of folklore in the phrase, "Who will make the child's death" [line 78], for there is said to have been that sort of sculpting technique—making figures of bread which assume their intended expression when they become hard—in rural areas of Bohemia. But it seems to me entirely unimportant whether Rilke was really thinking of such a custom.) The word "or" (line 79) confirms the fact that we have correctly characterized the drift of the image's sense. The image makes a leap: first death is *made*, and now one *leaves* death in the round mouth of the child "like the core of a lovely apple" (lines 79–81). What the poet is now evoking is the characteristically frightened expression which the child assumes when, while eating, it is unable to get something down its throat. The point of this is the holding on to it. The child does not want to relinquish what it is choking on, a measure of how much it regards the bitter and the sweet as belonging together. Both metaphors evidently aim at expressing that relationship of unity, so unimaginable for us, in which a child willingly accepts death. To us death seems imaginable only as the violent enemy to whom one cannot acquiesce. Thus: murderer.

If the fourth elegy's uniformly maintained theme, as it was posed in the initial question: when is our feeling ever undivided? has by means of the principle of mythopoetic inversion repeatedly opened up for us the way to understanding in detail, the tenth elegy, which Rilke himself thought the most successful, is dominated in its entire structure by this principle. Here one can lead the interpretation especially deeply into the re-translation. Nonetheless we will, in what follows, proceed merely summarily.

The theme which is sounded with the first invocation is the meaning of pain for human life and the perversity in our attitude toward pain. Right in this invocation in the proem we encounter a wonderful mythopoetic inversion; the nights are characterized as inconsolable sisters (lines 7–8), i.e., they are united with the speaker in the manner of brother and sisters, as if inconsolable, instead devoting themselves entirely to their pain. It is of course we human beings who by night devote ourselves entirely to our pain, because we can no longer take flight into any sort of distraction. Fear of the night, which they have who are pursued by sorrow or pain, is one of Rilke's basic motifs, especially in *The Notebooks of*

Malte Laurids Brigge, the first of his works to attain the level of his mature works.

Rilke calls us "wasters of pain" (line 10), i.e., we are uneconomical with that which we need constantly and which is indispensable for us. This is not the place to consider in its own right the theme of pain and its differentiation from joy. But everyone knows that pain drives one inward and for just that reason deepens. A face transformed by joy is certainly a thing of wonder, but pain alone leaves its mark on a face. This points toward the inner affinity of pain to life, to consciousness, to self-knowledge. The constant presence of pain can be heard, right down to the vocalization, in the line "site, settlement, camp, ground, dwelling-place" ("Stelle, Siedlung, Lager, Boden, Wohnort"—line 15), which enunciates a presence ever more deeply droning and thus ever more permanent.

Instead of this we see how little room pain still has in our human existence. This is shown by the complete deceitfulness of the cemetery at the edge of the city (line 20), and once more it is the angel, the being that knows no half emotions, no division in feeling, before whom none of this supposed sorrow would remain (he would trample it "without a trace" [line 20]). Thus the bitter phrase "market of consolation" (ibid.), where through the funeral home we replace, as it were, the symbolism of sorrow by money. One need only think of the Greek funerary steles, which in ever growing numbers are exhibited in the National Museum in Athens, to realize by the contrast that the monuments of our cemeteries are truly "the effusion of the casting-mould of emptiness" (line 18).

As suffering has here only a deceptive, repressed, marginal position, real life is for people a sort of constant fun-fair, the hunt for happiness and for the illusion of freedom, which drown out all thoughts of suffering. Without dealing in detail with the depiction of this fun-fair of life, it is quite clear what really counts in this life of deceit: success and money. Things begin to get serious for people at the point where money is at issue. That is here evoked by the phrase (line 29) "for adults": money (like sex) is something about which one does not actually talk, and yet is the thing which everyone is after. This fun-fair is fenced in, and posters for the beer "Deathless" hang on the boards of the fence. In this manner we have impressed on us once more that it is the sense of the whole fun-fair to act as if there were no death. Thus, if one chews on fresh distractions along with this beer, this means: one deadens the thought of death by hurling oneself into distractions.

It is only behind the fun-fair of life, in which everything is deceptive glitter, that one encounters the true emotions: children at play, lovers completely lost in one another, dogs that have for once been freed from their constant human captivity, and here the youth is drawn further on (line 41). The emphasis lies on 'youth'. Youths are, so the poem intimates, not yet as reasonable as adults. They are still wasteful with their feelings, are still capable of not getting over something, of confessing to themselves that something is not right and that one should not resign oneself to that fact. For them money is not yet so fascinating, and thus lamentation still exists for them. Once again it is mythopoetic inversion when the youth follows the [personified] Lament (lines 41 ff.), as if attracted by her—he follows her, touched by something which enchants him, until he finally turns back to the seriousness and reality of life. No longer may he, melancholic and unsuccessful, hang on to the thought of the perversity of reality, and so he gives up lamenting.

But then—as if this were merely a further episode in a unified narrative—the young deceased are spoken of, with whom things are different. They do not turn back, instead following the Lament. We shall understand nothing here unless we see that it is not the dead who follow the Lament, rather it is the lament of the bereaved which follows the dead, especially the young dead. Here lamenting is still as it were legitimate, so that nobody can blame a person who openly declares his loyalty to the Laments.

Now the poet constructs the mythical world of the Laments into which the deceased enters, and certainly from this point on one should not counterfeit as a frosty allegory something which is not collated feature by feature, but rather enchanted as a whole. Still it remains clear that the poet is speaking here of the lamentation for the deceased, and indeed in a manner such that the deceased appears as a subject of the proceedings in that he is with the Lament intended for him. If the Lament behaves with girls otherwise than with lads, then we may sense in this once again something of the difference in nature of men and women with respect to lamenting. If the Lament walks in silence with lads, then this has in it something to the effect that the lad does not give himself as freely as a girl to lamentation. That is the way one is supposed to see it.

The poet follows the young deceased into the realm of lamenting. What he shows first of all is that lamenting has lost its place in our world. The Laments are impoverished: "Once we were rich" (line 61). It is one of the elder Laments who knows about that. This too has its human dimension. The place of the young Lament gets taken by this elder, who points further up into the mountains, her homeland, and these mountains are no longer mountains of lamentation, but rather of suffering, i.e., of lamentation grown silent, hollowed out or like anger that has become petrified in slag. What is behind this is so to speak the whole inner dimension of pain, which leads from the externality of the audible lament to the most inner reality of a suffering which has become completely one with the person.

The elder Lament, who still knows something about the legitimacy of pain and lamenting in human existence, now leads the young deceased as it were through the archaeology of the land of suffering (lines 62 ff.). She shows him the ruined remains of a splendid dominion of suffering and lament. Ethnology and the history of religion allow us at once to fill that out with content, and in our times lament still rules in rurally cohesive areas: wailing women and all the rites of lament which belong to the funeral cult. The high poetic power of these verses conjures up for us a landscape of lamentation, in which tears are elevated to high tear-trees and whole fields of melancholy are in bloom, blossoms which in our world decorate a windowsill here and there merely as unusual foliage, i.e., they touch our lives only occasionally and at the edges. And when the grazing animals of sorrow are shown to the young deceased, here too no allegorizing individual interpretation is called for. Instead one has to feel how the silhouette of a herd grazing in the evening moves downhill and radiates sorrow.

At last night comes (line 73), and what is now depicted has an Egyptian quality to it, though of course we are not supposed to think that this landscape of lamentation is Egypt. What is shown here is not on the Nile. The Egyptian theme is sounded because this is the culture in which the dead have the greatest presence. But what are we meant to understand when another Sphinx rises here in the moonlight to the wonder of the young deceased, as Rilke once, in a marvellous letter, described his experience of the Egyptian Sphinx?[12] "The countenance of the secret chamber" (lines 76–77) certainly means the grave of the Pharaoh, over which the giant body with the human face has been erected. We can feel with the poet the breathtaking quality that emanates from the enormity of this petrified face, when the mobile, ever-changing and so vividly familiar quality of the human countenance now towers above the observer immersed in the light of eternity. Breathtaking, that this fleeting human life should weigh at all in the scale of the stars (lines 79–80). But what is meant with all this? At this point we are aided by the order of construction of the whole. A clear intensification leads us to this tomb: a royal head. It is the majesty of death, who here represents the Lord of all beings, the greatest pain of all and the greatest of all losses, and who thus gives the death-lament its rank. Here is the actual origin of lamentation.

So the poetic description of the young deceased's encounter with death is also determined by the incomprehensibility of death. Once again we have to invert: the young deceased, who—dizzy with his early death (lines 81–82)—is unable to

---

[12]The letter is reprinted in Steiner, 1962, in the commentary to lines 77 ff. of this elegy.

grasp the majestic tomb, stands for the incomprehensibility, for us who survive, of an early death. We do not know how to grasp it. None of this is made explicit in the mythic self-forgetfulness which the poet here maintains right through the entire description of a sweeping journey through the land of the Laments. For everthing remains a description of what is seen. Not until the owl flies up do we become fully aware of the size of this royal countenance; a page has to be enlarged by twice being unfolded from our usual quarto into folio size for us to take in the whole outline of the incomprehensible (lines 83–88).

If one looks higher still—that is how the beginning of the next strophe is meant—then one catches sight of the stars of the land of sorrow. The explainers, above all Steiner in his recent efforts, have taken pains to interpret particular ones among these constellations. It is very questionable whether this is even a correct task. One must rather think here of the poetic function of such precision, as the new semantics of literary studies has begun to recognize. As one there recognizes, e.g., 'lie-signals', so too we find here the signs of an entire experiential dimension of pain which we have denied. Surely any individual interpretation must meet the challenge that the new stars are stars of the land of sorrows. The symbols must have something to do with sorrow, and it seems to me to be the task to feel the whole of this rising firmament from the depths of the sorrow content attached to the individual symbols. Of course a constellation can also mirror by inversion the world of sorrows, as in, say, the happiness of the Cradle (line 93) or the blessed unity of man and animal in the Rider.—One of the *Sonnets to Orpheus* is able to express this theme.[13] But there the blessed union lasts only a fleeting moment, and even with the return home the disintegration of the union becomes tragically tangible when manger and table separate

---

[13][Rilke, 1942. Gadamer presumably means the eleventh sonnet of part one—Eds.]

horse and rider.[14]—If one wants to describe quite generally the direction of these star-symbols, the intensification that is to be found in their depiction will give the most important hermeneutical clue. This intensification suddenly becomes understandable in the 'M' which stands for 'the Mothers'. That can no longer be misunderstood: the constellation of the Mothers, which dominates the entire southern sky, represents the deepest experience of sorrow and of lamentation. It is maternal sorrow. In this manner we could say about each of the constellations of the land of sorrows a few things which awaken reminiscences and resonances, but it seems to me not in accordance with the poet's wish to try to determine origins when on the whole the orientation—and therewith the direction to look for understanding—is clearly marked.

Let us now follow the conclusion of the poem, i.e., let us complete the journey which the young deceased makes with the Lament, whom he finally leaves behind as he strides on alone into the Mountains of Primal Suffering (line 105). In mythopoetic inversion this journey of the young deceased through the landscape of the Laments means that whoever is engrossed in pain over a young deceased experiences in the blessing of lamentation the wisdom of the old lament-cultures. And when the Lament has to halt at the end of the journey so as to point from afar to the Springs of Joy, shimmering in the moonlight (lines 99–100), the sudden insight responds in us that at the end of lamentful mourning joy will once more spring up in the mourner. The Lament must leave the young deceased at the foot of the Mountains of Sorrow. When the laments fall silent, then the Lament is from that point on no longer with the young deceased. She accompanies him no longer.—That is: he now belongs so much to those

---

[14][Rilke actually speaks, in the 1942 edition, of horse and rider being separated by "*Tisch und Weide*," i.e., "table and pasture." Whether Gadamer had in mind some earlier version we do not know. In any event the sense of what he says fits quite well to the printed version of the eleventh sonnet—Eds.]

whose loss we learn to get over. The sorrow of relatives and others left behind is finally muted, turned as it were to stone in the heart. Thus the young deceased now strides on into the mountains alone.

Now he belongs to the endlessly dead (line 107) whom no remembrance, much less lamentation, ever calls back. But it is precisely those who are so endlessly dead who are supposed to "awaken a parable" in us (ibid.). This expressly signals the fact that there is something to be understood here. The long journey of the Lament with the young deceased is not without meaning and purpose. It leads to an insight, and this is the insight toward which the whole poetic invocation of the *Elegies* points: "That I may someday, at the close of the grim insight,/ sing joy and praise to the assenting angels" (lines 1–2). 'Assent' is the key which connects the tenth elegy with the first ("the appearance of injustice"—I, lines 66–67).

The poet makes a comparison here, and where things are compared it is certainly allowable to understand what the comparison means. The tails (or aments) of the bare hazel (lines 108–9) appear before the green leaves. The bush is still empty. But even a hazel bush which bears female blossoms can nonetheless never fertilize itself. The hazel is thus a symbol for something which blossoms not for itself, but rather squanders itself selflessly. In this it resembles the fertile spring rain (line 110), which also does not intend the fertility which it disseminates. And now the poem says that we should also see the young deceased in this manner. If we feel somehow moved, we are no longer filled with the accusation that here a life has not been lived out, and that the expectation of happiness which begins with each life has been disappointed. Rather, what is supposed to fill us with emotion is the fact that, contrary to our expectation, that too can be happy which does not find its self-fulfillment. And that is an assent which means more than that one reconciles oneself with the death of the young person. It is, as it were, impressed on us by the dying child, which has exemplified it for us in its whole undivided childlikeness.

The mythopoetic inversion which we have used as the hermeneutical key to the understanding of the *Elegies* had in Rilke's poetry an object of a special kind. The myth of that poetry is not myth (i.e., not a traditional saga) that is given a new poetic form. Nor is it a poetizing of the world which takes place here. On the contrary, it is precisely that which is the unpoetic in our world that is made the object of literary statement. Where is there a poetry of high style that could allow itself a line such as the one about the Post Office on Sunday, about which it is said that it is "shut" (line 22)?[15] But this is precisely the point: the poet, proceeding from the experience of his own heart, finds this actual world—in which myth no longer unites and the lamentation of the elegy is able to say powerfully the wrong and incorrect thing—still full of miracles. It is this overwhelming experience, so contrary to the *Zeitgeist*, which enables him to go beyond himself to talk about, and in the presence of, the angel—a mythopoetics of his own heart. I characterize it as mythopoetic inversion when the interpreter retranslates into his own categories of understanding that which the poet has in this manner reflected outwards. Certainly there is the threat of scholasticizing here. Thus it would be an incorrect scholasticism if one were to try everywhere to make the principle of mythopoetic inversion explicit, instead of following it. The explicit consciousness of it can only have the function of leading to a sort of hermeneutical self-purification by teaching us to recant the methodology of scholarly distancing, which deals with poetry as with every other object of our knowledge. But this means to regain, as meaningful and speaking, that text which seemed to conceal itself as alien and strange. All interpretation can but bring about a vibration of the sounding board from which the poetic melody is sung for us more vividly. Whatever interpretive explications serve this intention must simultaneously

---

[15][Rilke's word is *zu*, from *zugemacht* or *zugeschlossen*. Its use here in a list of adjectives by Rilke is at least highly colloquial, if not ungrammatical, hence Gadamer's remark about "poetry of high style"—Eds.]

sublate[16] themselves. Having worked out its horizon of understanding, one should one day read a poem in such a way that all explications are completely melted away by the unambiguous clarity with which the poem now states itself.

In this generality, however, the principle of poetic inversion applies to all poetry. A retranslation must always be possible, one which allows what is present in the lines to become present for us. In this sense 'parousia' is the name not only of a theological, but also of a hermeneutical, concept. 'Parousia' means nothing else but presence—and presence through the word, and only through the word, and in the word, that is what one calls: a poem.

---

[16][Since Hegel the ambiguous German verb *aufheben*—here rendered 'sublate'—has been used by philosophers to express simultaneously the notions of abolishing, preserving and elevating—Eds.]

3

Walther von der Vogelweide's Lyric of Dream-Love and Quasar 3C 273

Reflections on the so-called "circle of understanding" and on the so-called "theory-ladenness" of observations

WOLFGANG STEGMÜLLER

Passing a construction site one will often notice that some workers are standing around with nothing to do. Hasty Central Europeans are then wont to raise an eyebrow—at least in spirit—and murmur a few words about the decline of the work ethic during building booms. This is a typical *prejudice.* For in truth something quite different is going on. Although I am no friend of essential definitions, I still would answer a query about the *essence of human planning* in this manner: "it belongs to the essence of human planning that somebody or other has always got to wait for something or other." Prejudices are often very hard to overcome. This shows itself in our example, whose situation is mirrored on a higher level and in much greater dimensions in countries with centrally administered economies. For decades Marxist practitioners (and not only they) have waged a struggle as dogged as it is hopeless against the truth that misplanning is a constitutive element of planning. Nonetheless Marxist utopians right down to the present day seem blind to this truth.

Prejudices are an *impediment to knowledge* both in everyday life and in science, at least if one understands the word 'prejudice' in its ordinary sense. But the question is precisely whether there are not *certain types of prejudices* which are first of all *insuperable* and, secondly, *not to be evaluated negatively* because in them a basic feature of the human mind, a "prejudice-structure" of human understanding, is said to find expression. Ever since the hermeneuticist Ast made use of the metaphor (which Schleiermacher later took and entitled "the hermeneutical principle")[1] that "just as the whole is understood from the individual, so too the individual can only be understood from the whole," the tendency has been to answer both questions positively. Today people say, referring especially to Heidegger, that this circle has an *ontologically positive meaning*,[2] and that the subjectivity which manifests itself in it is a distinguishing and defining mark of the humanities (*Geisteswissenschaften*) as opposed to the "objective natural sciences."

Opponents of [philosophical] hermeneutics have repeatedly pointed to the dubious historical background of hermeneutical theories of understanding, e.g., to the fact that they are of theological origin and are thus themselves only secularized theology; that they arose with the Christian notion that human beings are distinguished from all other creatures in the universe by their immortal souls; and that later the Cartesian myth and/or the Hegelian metaphysics of spirit found their way into hermeneutical thinking.

All these things I intend to leave completely aside; for they concern only the *genesis* of a philosophical position and this is *never* decisive for its *correctness or incorrectness.*

I will restrict my attention to the phenomenon of the hermeneutical circle. *For the circle of understanding seems to be the rational core which remains after we eliminate all irrational factors from the thesis of the distinction or special position of the humanities vis-à-vis the natural sciences.* This too would not necessarily be a matter of importance, since it is open to doubt whether any division at all of the sciences has

---

[1]F. Schleiermacher, 1959/1977, p. 141/175 ff.

[2]H.-G. Gadamer in this volume, "On the Circle of Understanding," p. 71.

theoretical significance. But exactly this is what the hermeneuticists assert: the difference in the subject matter forces a difference in the method; analytical philosophy of science in particular is said to be inapplicable to humanistic disciplines because it ignores the circle of understanding.

Before one can test such a far-reaching assertion, one has to answer two questions of meaning: what actually is meant by 'hermeneutical circle'; and, equally, what is to be understood by its 'insuperability'? I shall try to discuss these questions without making reference to [philosophical] hermeneutics. In the following exposition I shall use the expressions 'hermeneutical' and 'understanding' solely as incomplete linguistic symbols in the context of 'hermeneutical circle' and 'circle of understanding', that is, solely as verbal aids to signify *a phenomenon still to be clarified.* As justification for such disregard of the hermeneutical literature I can only state in advance my conviction that the common phrase "the circle of understanding" is all wrong: The *definite article* is inappropriate, because we are not dealing with *one*, definite, sharply demarcated phenomenon; the expression '*understanding*' is out of place, since the 'circle of understanding' is not specific to any form of understanding at all; and the use of the word 'circle' is wrong too, because the 'circle of understanding' has nothing to do with a circle. Admittedly this designation in *one* of its meanings has something to do with the *mistaken impression* that we are faced with a circle here. To the extent that this is so, one must limit oneself to explaining how this impression arises and how it is possible for one to misinterpret it as a correct impression. It will, to be sure, turn out that the root of this impression is a genuine problem.

Although the following exposition will not deal with [philosophical] hermeneutics, I would still like at the start to list several difficulties for a logician trying to come to grips with hermeneutical literature.

(1) First there is the *pictorial-metaphorical* language of all the hermeneuticists. There is in itself nothing objectionable to the use of images, as long as those who use the images are aware that they are speaking in images. In this case this is

unfortunately almost never so: They use images and *think mistakenly* that they have spoken in precise concepts.

(2) Further there is the blurring of *object-* and *meta-levels*. I mention briefly an example: in his essay "Die Kunst der Interpretation" E. Staiger gave a reading of Mörike's poem "Die Lampe" ("The Lamp"). This then gave rise to a dispute with Heidegger which found expression in a published correspondence. The poem in question ends with the line: "Was aber schön ist, selig scheint es in ihm selbst." In order to contrast his opinion with Staiger's interpretation as clearly as possible, Heidegger makes a very reasonable suggestion: he translates the phrase "selig scheint es in ihm selbst" in two different ways into Latin. This suggestion can be called reasonable because the ancient Romans often expressed themselves much more clearly and unambiguously than we do in German (and this holds precisely in the present case,too). Heidegger proceeds from the determination that Staiger, in his interpretation, gives the phrase "selig scheint es in ihm selbst" the meaning of: "felix in se ipso (esse) videtur" (i.e., "(it) seems to be blissful in itself"—'selig' ('blessed', 'blissful') here construed predicatively and 'in sich selbst' ('in itself') as belonging to 'selig'—'felix'). Heidegger on the other hand takes the view—appealing *inter alia* to the 'pervasive' Hegelian aesthetic—that in the last line 'in ihm selbst' must go with 'scheint' ('seems', but also 'shines') and not with 'selig', and that 'scheint' must be interpreted in the sense of 'shines, gives light', so that the correct translation would run, "feliciter lucet in eo ipso" ("it shines blissfully in itself"). Staiger's reply contains among many other things the remarkable charge of conceptual scholasticism against Heidegger: "You seem to me, quite contrary to your own convictions, to insist too much on concepts, and to overlook the hovering, gliding, skittish, cautious [. . .] iridescent character of the sort of poetic speech Mörike cultivated."[3] He commits here the logical mistake of thinking that one can only talk in hovering, gliding, iridescent

[3]E. Staiger, 1955, p. 39.

speech *about* a poem that is composed in this kind of language. This mistake contradicts remarkably Staiger's own affirmation that interpretation has to be something other than "re-expression in prose." Of course a researcher (*Wissenschaftler*) *can and must talk* about a Mörike poem in clear concepts, and in addition be able to adopt a clear standpoint; or else he simply has to let it be. Heidegger had done nothing but contrast two incompatible interpretative hypotheses. He tried to clarify the different content of these hypotheses by means of the Latin translations, and gave his reasons for preferring the second hypothesis.

(3) Next and as an especially important point I cite the unclarity with respect to the status of the key hermeneutical concepts, i.e., concepts such as *understanding, prejudice, pre-understanding*. Consider, say, the expression 'prejudice'. We are here faced with the following alternatives:

First alternative: The word is *taken from everyday language*. This cannot be the case. Gadamer and others explicitly distinguish the *positive prejudice* from prejudice in the negative sense. But in everyday life this word is used *only* in the negative sense, in combination with 'against', not however in combination with 'for'. I have very often heard phrases of the sort, "N. N. has a prejudice *against* Americans, *against* Jews, or *against* Germans." I have never heard a phrase such as "N. N. has a prejudice *for* Eskimos, *for* Italians, or a prejudice *for* the Japanese."

Second alternative: the expression is a technical term introduced by explicit definition, which to be sure *sounds just like* a particular everyday word, but which does *not have the same meaning*, as the definition makes clear. Unfortunately this sort of definition is nowhere to be found.

Third alternative: one could take the view that we are dealing with a *theoretical* concept, which—rather like many basic physical concepts—eludes a sharp definition. I can respond to this sort of suggestion only with a Latin proposition, which possesses a negative celebrity in that it has *not* been articulated by *any* modern philosopher, although it *should* have been articulated long ago: "Termini sine theoria nihil valent" ("Terms without theory are worthless"). *What is this theory?*

(4) Another central hermeneutical concept is *understanding*. Dilthey's opposition of *understanding* and *explanation* seems to play a large role even today. The contrast between the natural sciences and the humanities is supposed thereby to be characterized as well as cemented. Of all the epistemological dichotomies that I know of (for example, 'analytic-synthetic', 'a priori-empirical', 'descriptive-normative', all of which prove more or less helpful *in certain contexts*) Dilthey's is *by far the least fruitful*. The reason for this has to do with the logic of language and concerns both of Dilthey's terms. First of all, in the case of 'understanding', this word is so equivocal that I am almost inclined ironically to employ a phrase of the early Wittgenstein, the author of the *Tractatus Logico-Philosophicus*, and say, "Understanding fills the whole of logical space." One can hardly conceive of a scientific activity to which the word 'understanding' could not be applied in a variety of ways and nonetheless quite adequately. Thus it is indeed correct to stress that literary scholars and historians are concerned to *understand* texts (or to *interpret them with understanding*); that they take pains to *understand* motives and character traits of historical personalities; that they attempt to *understand* cultural notions of norms and values. But one can immediately parallel such assertions with quite analogous statements about the activities of mathematicians and physicists. A student of these two disciplines must above all take pains to *understand* the fundamental principles of mathematics and physics. Later he must proceed to *understand* theorems, theories, and hypotheses. And for that it will prove necessary to come to *understand* the proofs given for the theorems and the arguments given for the hypotheses. This parallel surely does not show that mathematics and physics are *also* 'to be interpreted hermeneutically', but rather nothing more than that, on account of its numerous meanings and shades of meaning, the word 'understanding' contributes nothing to an account of the nature of the individual sciences and their relationship to one another. If we want to differenti-

ate and recognize distinctions, then we must not use as our 'key' an expression from which *some* meaning or other applicable to *any* situation at all can be squeezed.

The matter is made worse by the unfortunate fact that the word 'explain' is also exceptionally equivocal. Thus it is admittedly true that natural scientists often employ the so-called subsumption model of explanation and say, for instance; "The Galilean law of free fall and Kepler's laws can be explained at least approximately by the Newtonian Theory." But then again one can pick out other uses of 'explain' and with their help describe interpretative activity. Thus a linguist *explains* to us the meaning of words from a language we do not know; or a Sinologist *explains* to his audience the meaning of a Chinese poem. Therefore *either* the two expressions "understanding" and "explanation" signify totally *disparate* concepts, as for instance in "understanding a text—explanation of the law of free fall"; in that case the contrast is just as uninteresting and unfruitful as in other cases of disparate concepts: we expect no fundamental insights from a contrast of such concepts as prime number and parrot; *or* else the meaning-contents overlap. In that case one can formulate *a question which seeks understanding* in such a way that it becomes a question *asking for an explanation*, as for example in the three cases we saw, in which someone *does not understand* a concept, a theory, or a proof and *would like to have it explained.* It is similar in the question of analyzing the function of an automaton. Thus someone can say, "I *don't understand* the copying and transmission automatism of the genetic code; can someone *explain* it to me?" The two meanings are interlinked even in the question-and-answer game of moral accusation and justification, as when one says to the other, "I *don't underatand* how you could do such a thing. Can you *explain* your behavior to me?"

(5) I personally find the following extraordinarily disturbing: present-day hermeneuticists like to assure us repeatedly that they have *thoroughly liberated* themselves from the *psychologism* of Schleiermacher and the younger Dilthey. And *in the same breath* they employ phrases that can only be

interpreted psychologistically. Thus they speak of *acts* of understanding or of the accomplishment of understanding and the like. I know of only very few (and these only very unimportant) meanings of the word 'understanding' which make sense in such phrases. For the most part they are simply linguistically incorrect. In order to *understand* how this state of affairs came about we must probably have recourse to a quite different tradition from that of Schleiermacher and Dilthey: many, if not most, of today's hermeneuticists are in one way or another influenced by Heidegger and/or phenomenology, and for this reason they are spiritual descendants of F. Brentano, whose *doctrine of intentionality* continues to have a strong influence right down to the present. Brentano said what he meant with greater clarity and openness than his later progeny: intentional acts (of imagining, judging, willing, etc.) are acts of the 'mental agent', i.e., *what I would call the second, invisible person in the visible person.* Brentano's theory of consciousness is *a variant* of the opposing theory which Wittgenstein used as a foil for the demarcation of his own philosophy of the mental. (I remind the reader of such Wittgensteinian statements as that our language makes us suspect a physical occurrence, we find none, and thereupon invent an invisible mind; for 'to think' and 'to imagine' have the same grammar as 'to run').

(6) The greatest difficulty concerns the question of the analysis of examples. To the extent that we leave aside the interpretation of religious texts and therefore hermeneutics in the theological sense, one must unfortunately say that *such analysis of examples is totally absent.* One would surely expect that authors who write voluminous works and lengthy treatises on hermeneutics or on the difference between natural scientific and humanistic knowledge would show by means of concrete historical or literary examples how a humanities scholar, as distinguished from a natural scientist, *formulates* his hypotheses, how he places them *in logical relationships to one another*, how he *argues for his theses*, and how he *defends them against the criticisms and attacks of other-minded colleagues.* In this respect there is without doubt a gulf be-

tween natural philosophy and philosophy of science concerned with so-called 'natural scientific knowledge', on the one hand, and hermeneutics on the other. While the one group at least tries to elucidate and to clarify its abstract considerations by means of example—whether it be simplified models, or else analysis of existing theories in natural science and their applications—the analogue to this is altogether absent.

We now return to our theme proper.

I shall distinguish six different meanings of the phrase 'hermeneutical circle', without however thereby making a claim to completeness. In each of these meanings we are faced with a specific form of a *dilemma*:

(I) *the dilemma of interpretation of one's own language*;
(II) *the dilemma of the interpretation of foreign languages*;
(III) *the problem of the theoretical circle*;
(IV) *the dilemma of the standpoint-dependence of the observer*;
(V) *the dilemma of confirmation*;
(VI) *a dilemma in the differentiation of background knowledge and facts*.

The first four problem-types shall be dealt with only briefly, the last two, however, in detail.

To exclude any misunderstanding, I expressly point out that this list intentionally contains only such interpretations of "hermeneutical circle" as characterize definite types of *difficulties* for the fields of learning which are affected by them. No doubt there are as well other interpretations which are *harmless* in the sense that in them the attempt is made graphically to call attention to some more or less interesting phenomenon, which leads to no special epistemological difficulties and contains furthermore nothing specific to humanities scholarship. An example of this would be an aspect of what Carnap calls the *explication of a concept*. What is here at issue is a typical case in which *intuitive 'pre-understanding'* enters into what is in the end to be obtained, i.e., the explicated concept (*Explikat*), and indeed in such a way that one can say: what emerges in the end contains neither an abandonment nor an overcoming, but rather a *working out*, of the original pre-understanding. Unlike Carnap, who represented this process as one of linear progress from vagueness to precision, I would tend rather to see in conceptual explication a process with reiterated negative feedback, since a successful explication will depend on repeated recurrence to, and revisions of, the intuitive basis.[4] One could try to represent this process pictorially as a *spiral*, where the gradient is a gauge for the increase of understanding gained in the course of the explication. Perhaps one or the other hermeneuticist has meant something of this sort with the 'circle of understanding'.

The image of the '*hermeneutical spiral*' is applicable wherever an *increase* of understanding comes about, on the one hand, while on the other this gain is achieved *not without considerable effort*. There is no reason to assume that this image is applicable only for definite sorts of scholarly work in the humanities. In particular it applies *as well to metatheoretical interpretations*, and indeed to such as refer to *natural scientific* theories. For it must be stressed, against a widely held opinion, that, as far as a deeper understanding of natural scientific theories is concerned, here too we are still at the beginning. So the image of the spiral is multiply applicable. One must, to be sure, not forget that in all these applications it is still *only an image*.

But let us return now to the difficulties we listed. A few of them, i.e., (I) and (II), are found only in disciplines which are traditionally labeled as humanities. But what holds of them is no more than that they *can* arise, not however that they *have to*. Others, e.g., (IV) and (V), are presumably not limited to particular branches of study at all. Finally, the last difficulty (VI) occurs only in fields of study of a definite formal type, which however do not need to belong to the humanities.

---

[4]Compare W. Stegmüller, 1976, Introduction (Section IV); and 1973a, pp. 25 f.

(I) *The dilemma of interpretation of one's own language*: formulated abstractly, this problem—which occurs only in certain, and by no means in all, cases—can be put roughly like this: *in order to be able to interpret a particular text formulated in the language of the interpreter, one has to proceed from an assumption about the intention of the author*—I want to call this assumption the major hypothesis—*which can prove to be false in the course of the reading*. In the resulting task of replacing with a better one the major hypothesis which has been rejected in the course of the reading, we run into the following difficulty: *the correct major hypothesis could only be attained by a successful study of just that text which itself can only be read with understanding by taking this still unavailable major hypothesis as our basis*.

To illustrate what only seems to be a complicated situation I shall employ a particularly topical example from my own language: the *Philosophische Untersuchungen* (*Philosophical Investigations*) by L. Wittgenstein (Wittgenstein, 1953). Although this masterpiece of German prose contains not a single technical term, reading it proves uncommonly difficult. What is the cause of this difficulty?

Wittgenstein very often develops his ideas in the form of a dialog with an imaginary opponent, whose views he quotes literally and then answers. I assume that most readers will have the same experience as I at the first reading: whatever Wittgenstein's opponent says always seems to be correct, while Wittgenstein's responses seem in part incomprehensible, in part absurd. This impression is especially strong in those passages in which Wittgenstein polemicizes against the view that it is possible for language to refer to private sensations.

At a further stage the reader realizes that his difficulty in comprehending may be due to the fact that Wittgenstein is advocating a theory of the meaning of linguistic expressions which differs completely from the traditional view. Wittgenstein connects the concept of the meaning of a word directly with that of the use of a word. The reader does not recognize this connection. Here we have already reached the core of the difficulty which I have called the dilemma of interpretation within one's own language: In order to read the *Philosophische Untersuchungen* with genuine understanding, the reader would have to know Wittgenstein's theory of meaning. But he can become acquainted with this theory in no other way than by an appreciative study of just this book. This is a genuine difficulty. It has this formal structure:

> "To understand A one would first have to know B; to acquire knowledge about B, one would first have to understand A."

This is, as I said, a genuine difficulty, but it is a *dilemma*, not a *circle*. The difficulty is certainly not insuperable in principle: competing interpretative hypotheses can be scrutinized on the basis of various criteria such as: inner consistency, agreement with as many passages in the text as possible, logical connection and coherence of the interpretation's constituent parts, agreement with independent knowledge about the author, etc. If at the end, after eliminating inadequate hypotheses, there are still several open possibilities, then this can (but need not) be due to a lack of information. It is in any case *not* due to the nature of the thing itself. With the expression, "If there are still several open possibilities, then this need not be due to a lack of information," I wanted to hint at the thesis that not only can one understand an author better than the author himself, but also that this 'understanding better' is possible in several ways.

If with their thesis of the indissolubility of the hermeneutical circle hermeneuticists are supposed to mean *the insuperability of this dilemma*, then one could not deduce from this a statement about the characteristic mark of knowledge in the humanities; the most that follows is the demand that all disciplines affected by this dilemma should close their doors, since their activity represents a hopeless undertaking.

Instead of proceeding from the radical alternative: "the dilemma is always superable—the dilemma is never superable," one will have to make a specific investigation in each concrete case. There will then be two possibilities: *either* one arrives at a solution in spite of the difficulty (in our example, a theory of the Wittgensteinian view of meaning)—in this case the dilemma is overcome and no longer exists; *or*, given the present information, the dilemma stands. In this case one must, at least temporarily, give up the hope of arriving at a serviceable theory (in our example: of being able to read the work with comprehension), and one can only hope that at some future date new empirical material or else luck, accident, and inspiration will show one the way out of the blind alley.

(II) *The dilemma of the interpretation of foreign languages*: another difficulty is similar, though in an important respect different. In its formal structure it is analogous to the preceding case. The difference from case (I) lies in the fact that the text to be interpreted is written, not in the interpreter's language, but in a *foreign language*, perhaps even one which has not for a long time been spoken on this planet. It is possible that a difficulty with this structure crops up much more frequently in the second case than in the first, i.e., we will—perhaps—be confronted much more frequently with *this* interpretation-dilemma. Habermas seems to have this difficulty in mind when he comes to speak of the phenomenon of the hermeneutical circle.[5] His idea is more or less as follows: if an interpreter wants to interpret texts of a bygone epoch, he has no access to the past way of life independently of those texts, for this way of life is irrevocably gone. So *supposedly* a circle arises: *the interpreter has to deduce the past way of life from the linguistic expressions handed down; on the other hand he needs a knowledge of this way of life to understand the language of the past.*

Here too we have, not a *circle*, but a *dilemma*. This dilemma is, however, not as big as the suggestion just made might lead one to believe. First of all, it is not true that we have access to a past way of life only via texts. One can gain interesting information about the behavior of people in past epochs from pictorial representations and findings of other

[5]Compare J. Habermas, 1968/1971, pp. 214 f./169.

sorts. Secondly, it is even incorrect to assert that what is here being called the way of life of past epochs is gone irrevocably. Old customs, e.g., wedding customs, have often continued right to the present. A folklorist who studies contemporary customs can therefore certainly be in a position to convey to the historian knowledge about particular modes of social behavior in the past.

But I do not want to spend any more time on the type of difficulties represented by interpretations (I) and (II). For although this dilemma, as one of *interpretation*, occurs only in interpretative humanistic research, the difficulties *with the stated formal structure* are by no means limited to the humanities. On the contrary, difficulties with this typical structure can occur in *all* branches of study. (So, to take our later example of the quasar phenomenon, one could cast its basic difficulty in a form with the same structure as the interpretation-dilemma, to wit: "In order to be able satisfactorily to interpret the quasar phenomenon, one would have to be in command of the proper cosmological model, but one could not attain an adequate cosmological hypothesis as long as no one has found a correct interpretation of the quasar phenomenon.")

(III) *The theoretical circle*: in recent discussions in the philosophy of science so-called *theoretical function concepts* (*Funktionsbegriffe*) and their puzzling nature have played an important role. While people were at odds for a long while on how to mark these concepts off, more recent investigations, especially by J. D. Sneed, suggest the idea of characterizing these concepts by the manner in which they function in the application of a theory. Here they occupy a highly remarkable position, for the values of these functions are *measured in a theory-dependent manner*. Roughly speaking, this means: in order to be able to determine *whether such a concept* belonging to a theory is applicable to a case, *one must already be familiar with successful applications of just this theory*. Here the danger of a circle really does arise—a genuine, vicious one. To avoid this danger Sneed draws quite drastic consequences, among others that a theory cannot be interpreted as a system of propositions.

The justification for mentioning this point at all in the present context lies in the fact that we are here too faced with a *circle of understanding* in that an 'understanding' of the theory in which the term occurs is presupposed.

But here too, and for the same reason as before, it appears inadvisable to consider this more closely *in the present context*. It *may* indeed be that we have here a situation somehow or other *analogous* to that which some hermeneuticists had in mind. But the problem in question appears wherever particular types of theoretical concepts are used. Perhaps it appears *only* in physics and maybe other natural sciences, at any rate, *not only* in humanistic disciplines. Thus, however interesting the problem is in itself, still it is not likely to belong in the present context from the point of view of all those philosophers who are prepared to subsume under the concept "hermeneutical circle" only such phenomena as represent potential candidates for distinguishing the humanities (or certain of them) from the natural sciences.

(IV) *The dilemma of the standpoint-dependence of the observer*: by the observer I here mean the historian or the interpreter, and *the thesis of the indissolubility of the hermeneutical circle* is equated with the assertion that this standpoint-dependence is irrevocable. The answer to this depends on what exactly is meant with it.

(1) One possible, very radical interpretation is the following: every interpretation of texts and every explanation of human actions presupposes a *pre-understanding*. And the interpreter can 'never quite escape' this pre-understanding in the sense that he makes use of certain presuppositions ('prejudices') which are not only *de facto* untested but which *he in principle cannot test*. So, tacitly or expressly, he makes a series of hypothetical assumptions which he in principle cannot subject to testing, and from which, therefore, *since* he is not able to test them, he is all the less able to liberate himself.

I could make only two comments to this kind of interpretation: first, the hermeneuticist who asserts something of this sort must carry the burden of proof for it. Secondly, I haven't the slightest idea how such a proof would look.

If this radical thesis nonetheless seems plausible, it is likely to be due either to a confusion of the concepts '*de facto* not tested' with 'in principle untestable' or else to a fallacious inference from the premise that we must—in all reasoning and interpreting—make some presuppositions or other (for without any presuppositions we could not even begin to reason) to the statement that there are untestable presuppositions. The last-named inference is fallacious because the following two statements are thoroughly compatible and hence both can be correct: (a) one cannot all at once discard, or even merely doubt, every presupposition; (b) one can subject every single one of these presuppositions to criticism and even, on the basis of this criticism, to revision.

(2) The so-called 'standpoint' might mean something like what T. S. Kuhn calls a 'paradigm'. A precise analysis of this view would require a detailed discussion of his conception of science, which is of course not possible here, so I must limit myself to a few suggestions. According to Popperians and other rationalist critics of Kuhn, the unprecedented aspect of his basic idea is that he imputes a completely irrational attitude to natural scientists (which is why, according to Lakatos, one could say that Kuhn replaces philosophy of science with applied mass psychology). Both forms of the scientific enterprise described by Kuhn seem to be characterized by the dominance of a nonrational attitude: the *normal scientist* uses his paradigm theory solely as an instrument for puzzle-solving, but he never subjects it to critical examination, instead uncritically holding onto it (like a narrow-minded dogmatist). And likewise *in times of scientific revolutions* a new theory is not developed because the old one ran afoul of experience (was empirically falsified). Instead *the new theory directly supplants the old*, in which process of supplanting what matters is not argument but rather conversion-experiences, persuasion, and propaganda.

It seems to me that Kuhn's analyses and historical illustrations represent the strongest challenge thus far to contemporary philosophy of science. I experience this challenge as especially large, since I am convinced that Kuhn is correct on the essential points. Thus I do not think one can deal with his challenge via 'rationalistic polemics' of the sort practiced by the Popperians. The issue is instead to come up with a rational reconstruction of Kuhn's concepts of *normal science* and of the phenomenon of the *immediate supplanting of one theory by another*. This is in fact possible. To be sure, one has to be prepared *to surrender certain stereotypes of rational scientific behavior*. For, you see, I feel that Kuhn has done for the philosophy of science exactly the opposite of what his critics accuse him of: instead of demonstrating the irrationality in the behavior of scientists, he has caught sight of *new dimensions of scientific rationality*.

In particular, the concept of scientific rationality must not be hitched to concepts such as those of severe test and corroboration (or confirmation). Rational reconstruction of the concept of normal science, for instance, takes place via *explication of a concept of holding a theory* according to which persons can hold one and the same theory and still connect with it the *most varied convictions and hypotheses*. From this viewpoint many of Kuhn's provocative utterances become not only intelligible but also justifiable, as for example his assertion that the only kind of theory-rejection to which counterexamples by themselves can lead consists in the *rejection of science as a profession*; for empirical failure is a reflection, not on the *theory*, but on the *person* who has command of it, or, as Kuhn puts it, the inability to find solutions for difficulties (anomalies) *discredits only the scientist and not the theory*.[6] The main reason why I do not want to spend more time on this point is the same as before: if what is meant by the hermeneutical circle is the 'inescapability of pre-understanding', and if this is thought to represent something analogous to what I just called 'having command of a theory in Kuhn's sense', then not only would the hermeneutical circle not be specific to the humanities and characteristic of them alone; what is more, it

---

[6]For details on the logical reconstruction of Kuhn's conception of science, compare W. Stegmüller, 1976.

would be a matter of something which has thus far been explicated with precision only for the exact natural sciences and which could be carried over to the case of the humanities at best in a secondary sense. Furthermore, the term 'circle' could be applied here at best metaphorically.

I would now like to proceed to the two possible interpretations (V) and (VI) of the hermeneutical circle; I shall discuss these two interpretations simultaneously because of their close connection.

Once more, what are at stake are particular kinds of difficulties to which I will give the names 'the confirmation dilemma', Problem (V), and 'the problem of distinguishing background knowledge from knowledge of facts', Problem (VI).

My reasons for concentrating mainly on these final two points, and among them especially on difficulty (VI), are the following: first, only Problem (VI) implies a dilemma affecting *historical* knowledge alone. Secondly, this is the only interpretation in which the phenomenon to be analyzed is connected with the *impression of a genuine circle.* Third, we shall see that the talk of the indissolubility of the hermeneutical circle is this time not only meaningful, but is in addition accurate; for *this final dilemma is in point of fact ineliminable.*

For the sake of greater vividness I shall briefly elucidate the difficulty with two examples, one drawn from German literature, the other from astrophysics.

The first example is taken from a case study analyzed in detail in Heide Göttner's book, *Logik der Interpretation.* It concerns a discussion between the two Germanists, Wapnewski and Hahn, over the correct interpretation of the poem by Walther von der Vogelweide 74, 20. This lyric of dream-love is reproduced here first in the original and then in translation.

WALTHER VON DER VOGELWEIDE

Nemt, frowe, disen kranz (74,20)

a I »Nemt, frowe, disen kranz«,
alsô sprach ich zeiner wol getânen maget,
»sô zieret ir den tanz
mit den schoenen bluomen, als irs ûffe traget.
het ich vil edele gesteine,
daz müest ûf iur houbet,
obe ir mirs geloubet.
sêt mîn triuwe, daz ichz meine.«

b II »Ir sît sô wol getân,
daz ich iu mîn schapel gerne geben wil,
so (i)chz aller beste hân:
wîzer unde rôter bluomen weiz ich vil,
die stênt sô verre in jener heide.
dâ si schône entspringent
und die vogele singent,
dâ suln wir sir brechen beide.«

c III Si nam daz ich ir bôt,
einem kinde vil gelîch daz êre hât.
ir wangen wurden rôt,
same diu rôse, dâ si bî der liljen stât.
Do (e)rschampten sich ir liehten ougen:
doch neic si mir schône.
daz wart mir ze lône.
wirt mirs iht mêr, daz trage ich tougen.

e IV Mich dûhte daz mir nie
lieber wurde, danne mir ze muote was:
die bluomen vielen ie
von dem boume bî uns nider an daz gras.
seht dô muost ich von fröiden lachen.
do (i)ch sô wünneclîche
was in troume rîche,
dô taget ez und muos ich wachen.

d V Mir ist von ir geschehen,
daz ich disen sumer allen meiden muoz
vast under d'ougen sehen:
lîhte wirt mir einiu, so ist mir sorgen buoz.
waz obe si gêt an disem tanze?
frowe, dur iur güete

rucket ûf die hüete!
owê g(e)sæhe ichs under kranze!

Translation (based on Hahn's modern German version)

I. "Accept this wreath, my lady," I said to a beautiful girl, "thou shalt be the adornment of the dance when you wear the lovely flowers. If I had a precious diadem, believe me, I would set it upon your head. You can trust what I say, I really mean it." (a)

II. "You are so lovely that I would like to give you the best wreath I have at my disposal: I know where there are many white and red flowers—out there on that heath. There, where they blossom in glory and the birds are singing, let us pick them together." (b)

III. She accepted what I offered quite like a young lady. Her cheeks blushed, as the rose glows beside the lily. Bashfulness crept into her bright eyes. Nonetheless a lovely bow was her answer. That was my payment. If I receive more, I shall keep it to myself. (c)

IV. It seemed to me I had never before been so happy as there: blossoms rained down from the tree on us in the grass. Lo, I had to laugh for sheer joy. Just when I was so deeply delighted—in my dream, day broke and I awoke. (e)

V. The way she treated me drives me to peer deeply into the eyes of all the girls this summer. Perhaps I shall find "her," then I shall be rid of all dark thoughts. What, suppose she were dancing right here? My ladies, be so kind as to lift your hats a touch! Ah, if I could see her with her wreath here before me! (d)

This poem, handed down in three manuscripts, presents a problem in that at first the reader is not able fully to grasp the thread. Since both the individual phrases and the individual stanzas all form per se intelligible units, the problem of finding the thread amounts to the *question of the correct succession of the stanzas*. At any rate the assumption that such a reduction is possible is the common presupposition of the two interpreters, and so I accept it here.

Many literary critics have agreed that the final two stanzas of the manuscript should be interchanged, that is, d must be placed after e, with the result that, instead of the dream motif and the awakening, the search for the girl is put at the conclusion. I have already taken this general agreement into account in my text. The following exposition thus always refers to the revised text of the poem.

It seems that we are dealing with a dance-song. In the first stanza the knight invites his lady to accept "disen Kranz" (this wreath) with his compliments. Curiously the lady makes no reply to this. Instead, the knight commences once more in the second stanza, i.e., he continues with further praise and mentions a—which? a new?—wreath, "the best of all he has." Apparently this wreath does not exist yet; rather he wants still to pluck, far from the place of the dance, the white and red flowers for the wreath. Only now does she accept. It is unclear what 'lon' (payment) in this stanza refers to. In the fourth stanza the love-rapture turns out in the end to be a dream illusion. According to the fifth and final stanza the consequence is said to be that the poet must in this summer peer into all the girls' eyes in order to find "her" again.

Given the aforementioned assumption, the problem is limited to the correct order of the second and third stanzas. It is here that two interpretative hypotheses crystallized.

The *first hypothesis*, Wapnewski's, shall be divided into four subhypotheses: the two foundation hypotheses, H1 and H2, which serve as auxiliary hypotheses for the main hypotheses, H3 and H4.

H1 claims that in the second stanza a different person is speaking from in the first. Stanza I is a knight's stanza, the second, however, a lady's; in the first stanza the speaker is the knight-suitor, in the second it is the courted lady.

H2 claims that stanza c belongs before b; i.e., the order of the second and third stanzas should be reversed.

This reversal-hypothesis H2 is indeed an immediate consequence of the first hypothesis; Wapnewski does not, however, base it on this sort of inference, but instead puts forward independent evidence in favor of his suppositions H1 and H2.

H3 is the *interpretative hypothesis* proper, which restores the initially missing thread. It consists of Wapnewski's proposed reading, which is best rendered in his own words:

I. Nemt, frowe (Accept, my lady)	(a) The knight offers a young beautiful girl, as is the custom, a wreath of flowers to wear in the dance. But, as he swears, he would rather adorn her head with gems.
II. Sie nam (She accepted)	(c) She accepts—and with a gesture which expresses her inner nobility. Her white cheeks blush, [. . .] her eyes are lowered in bliss and bashfulness. [. . .] She bows in thankfulness. [. . .] If more thanks is granted him, then he will, to be sure, treasure it in his heart.
III. Ir sît (You are)	(b) Now she responds: he too, the knight, is handsome. She too would like to give him a wreath. [. . .] The most beautiful thing she has saved she will give him. Far from here, on the heath where the birds are singing they will pluck flowers and she will give him the wreath.
IV. Mich dûhte (It seemed to me)	(e) There he is filled with the greatest bliss; and the blossoms waft down. In this moment [. . .] the break occurs: excess of bliss makes him laugh, and his laughter awakens him! This point shows that Walther has not in fact 'broken his word', his promise to keep the

	secret: [. . .] the whole encounter was only a dream.
V. Mir ist (The way she treated me)	(d) Now awake, the poet is driven to act still as the slave of his dream bliss: he seeks his beloved the whole summer. Perhaps he will meet her among the girls who are dancing before him? Would they please raise their headdresses a trifle? If only (and with that the poem's final line flows literally and pictorially back into the dream-world of the first stanza) he were to find her beneath the headdress!

The second main hypothesis H4 is a *literary historical hypothesis* concerning the poem's place in literary history. After very subtle individual investigations, which cannot be reproduced here, Wapnewski arrives at the conclusion that this poem is a so-called *pastoral.* According to his conviction Walther's song contains all the marks of this genre: "the encounter of a man and a girl leading to consummation. The locale is the open air; and apparently the time is spring. The social status of the two is very different, his is high (knight), hers is lowly (country lass). The hero of the incident is identical with the narrator (first-person form). The report encompasses as its kernel an erotic dialog."

(Whether a scholar directs his attention primarily to H3 or H4 depends on whether he is interested in the interpretation as such, or, like Wapnewski, is primarily interested in the historical classification.)

If H4 is correct, it would amount to a very interesting discovery in the history of literature. For one would have to assume, in contrast to earlier views, that Walther von der Vogelweide not only was familiar with pastoral poetry, he also was the first to attempt to introduce it in Germany.

The second interpretation comes from G. Hahn. I will label it the *counter-interpretation* to Wapnewski's. Wapnewski's four hypotheses are matched by four counter-hypotheses CH1 . . . CH4, while CH3 represents the counter-hypothesis in the narrow sense. This counter-interpretation rests upon a thorough criticism of Wapnewski's hypotheses. Hahn too presents a series of independent arguments about H1 and H2, not—in contrast to Wapnewski—reasons which support these hypotheses, but rather such as shake them, i.e., which support doubt about their correctness. As for hypothesis H4, Hahn presents, quite apart from the indirect criticism already contained in his arguments against its supporting base-hypotheses H1 and H2, direct arguments against Wapnewski's classification of Walther's lyric, especially the following: (1) in all other pastoral poetry the difference of estate (on the one hand a knight, on the other a country lass) is very sharply accentuated. In Walther's poem we can at most add the difference of estate in our imagination, it is not expressly stressed. (2) Walther's poem contains motifs alien to the pastoral, to wit those of the dance and the dream.

For anyone who finds these criticisms legitimate, Wapnewski's interpretation hypothesis H3 also collapses: the rejection of H1 and H2 already makes the interpretation-hypothesis H3 questionable, for these two hypotheses, H1 and H2, form the foundation on which H3 rests. Since for Wapnewski H4, the literary-historical hypothesis, was derived as an inference from H3, his interpretative hypothesis H3 is additionally shaken by the criticism of H4, and indeed independently of the prior criticism.

In the crucial point of difference Hahn's interpretation amounts to the following: *in stanza b the suitor continues his speech, intensifying it.* In order to be able to carry this thought consistently through, Hahn must assume that in the poem no less than three wreaths are being spoken of: the only *real* one is the flower wreath offered to the girl in the first stanza; *unreal* is the diadem of gems mentioned by the suitor in his declaration; while the "best wreath of all," evoked in stanza b, is *potential*, left to the result of a decision still to be made.

As this example shows, we are faced with a highly peculiar

situation: even after evaluation of all the evidence as well as of the available philological and literary-critical analyses of this evidence; further, after consultation of all literary and cultural-historical knowledge, and after working out the symbolic meanings of the expressions and phrases employed; and finally after comparison with the rest of Walther's work and even the whole of German and non-German lyric poetry, and much more—even after evaluating all this—we seem to be confronted with a *dilemma of confirmation: every argument in favor of Wapnewski's hypothesis can be met with a counterargument that speaks for Hahn's alternative hypothesis.*

The following question is now obvious: should we perhaps understand by 'hermeneutical circle' this dilemma of confirmation? or, more precisely, its consequence, *that in the final instance it is the subjective feeling of the interpreter which must tip the balance in favor of the one interpretation or the other*?

For in the natural sciences, it could be argued, no analogous dilemma can come up. Therein lies the *objectivity of natural scientific knowledge*: the student of nature would, in a similarly situated case think up an *experimentum crucis* whose outcome would force a falsification of the one, and thus a conclusive decision in favor of the other, hypothesis.

But things are not so simple. Even if we provisionally accept the quite problematical concept of the *experimentum crucis*, we must still remember that not in *all* natural sciences are we able *experimentally* to force decisions between competing alternative hypotheses. One science, which, just like history, must be satisfied with the given facts is *astronomy*. (It can never become an experimental science, since we cannot move the heavenly bodies around.) Let us also take from this discipline our second example, which exhibits in its *formal structure* a certain parallel to the example from German literary criticism.

As even many nonastronomers realize, there has been more excitement in this discipline in the past eighteen years than in the whole preceding century and a half. Among the most sensational discoveries were the *quasars*. A brief preliminary remark may illustrate the importance of this discovery: If we imagine our sun to be moved out of our planetary system into the position of one of the nearest fixed stars, the radio waves hitting the earth would be some hundred billion times weaker than today and thus quite impossible to detect. Consequently it created a sensation among the experts when five tiny stars, to wit of the 13th magnitude, were discovered in 1963, all within a short period, which were able to be identified with already known radio sources. The term 'quasars' was coined for them, an abbreviation of 'quasi-stellar radio sources'. They were a puzzle to the researchers for a second reason, in addition to their *intense radio waves*: their light was strong enough for analysis into its spectral colors in the usual manner. Every chemical element, as is well known, has its characteristic lines which show up in a quite definite place in the spectrum. However, the quasar-spectrums could not be interpreted in this manner. One had indeed reason to believe that these luminous objects were surrounded by gas; but this gas seemed to be completely unknown. Not until several years later did it turn out that we were dealing with nothing other than the most common element in the universe, hydrogen. There was a very simple reason why the hydrogen lines had not previously been recognized as such: the lines were located not where one should have expected them, but were shifted quite far into the red part of the spectrum.

This *extraordinarily strong red-shift* greatly puzzled the astronomers. And here we have already the formal analogy to the Walther example. Just as in that case the *presupposed background knowledge*—I want to speak of the *major hypothesis of the context of meaning* (*Sinnzusammenhang*)—combined with other accepted knowledge allowed only two possible interpretations, so too in the present case the *available physical background knowledge*—or, as we can also say, the *major physical hypothesis*—allowed only two possible interpretations. Put briefly, this major hypothesis says: *red-shifts can come about in only two ways.*

Let us briefly consider these two alternatives analogously to the first example:

First alternative: it could be the case that light from these sources has to start off against a very strong field of gravity and thereby loses energy; red light, however, has less energy than blue.

The appraisal of this first interpretative possibility is based on a hypothesis which was in fact verified in 1967: the hypothesis of the existence of so-called *neutron stars*. Thus the first hypothetical alternative consisted in the assumption *that a quasar is a neutron star* (*local gravitation hypothesis*). Here we would indeed have the "struggle of light against a gravitation field" to which we would have to impute the strong red-shift. For these stars have an enormous density: one cubic centimeter has a density on the order of a billion tons.

However, considerable misgivings were immediately raised. I cite two crucial difficulties: neutron stars have a diameter of around ten kilometers. Since quasars are visible as stars of the thirteenth magnitude, their *distance from us could at most be 0.3 light-years*, if indeed they are neutron stars. Thus they would practically be within the bounds of our planetary system, and would disturb the planetary orbits so greatly that we would not have to have waited for today's precision instruments to detect these disturbances; indeed, Kepler would already have to have noticed them in the seventeenth century. Secondly, the place of the quasars in the heavens remains totally unchanged during the earth's entire revolution around the sun. From this fact we can conclude *that they are at least 6,000 light-years away*.

Second alternative: the other remaining possibility claims that the red-shift of the hydrogen lines in the quasars' spectrum is to be attributed to the so-called *Doppler effect*. According to it the quasars would be receding from the earth at extraordinarily high speeds, which in certain cases would approach the speed of light.

Now, however, from this recessive speed together with the relative constancy of the quasars' celestial position during the earth's revolution around the sun,[7] we can conclude that even

[7]Their place in the heavens has been constant during the entire fifteen years since the discovery of the first quasars.

the nearest quasar must be at least two billion light-years away (*cosmological hypothesis*). The physico-astronomical background knowledge thus forces us to set up the alternative: *either the quasars are at most 0.3 light-years away, or they are at least two billion light-years away.*

The big problem with the second alternative is *the brightness of the quasars at these colossal distances*. This can only be explained by the supposition that the quasars have a *colossal mass*. So at first the conjecture emerged that these were perhaps '*super galaxies*', which are many, perhaps a hundred or even several hundred times larger than a middle-sized galaxy such as our Milky Way. This idea would also harmonize with the law of the general expansion of the Universe, according to which a galaxy recedes from the earth more rapidly the further away it is.

Unfortunately this conjecture soon collapsed. Independently of each other, American and Russian astronomers came to the conclusion, initially based on an analysis of the magnitudes recorded in the older star charts, that between the years 1896 and 1963 the brightness of the quasar 3C 273 changed by 0.7 magnitudes. Later investigations revealed variations of brightness even within several days. If it were a Milky Way, not to mention a super galaxy, light would require a hundred-thousand or several hundred-thousand years to traverse the quasar, so that variations of brightness would be observable only within such colossal temporal intervals. Thus one seemed forced to accept the conclusion that quasars must be celestial objects with a diameter of at most several light-days.

One can readily imagine why this outcome amounted to a colossal challenge for astronomy. It had previously been assumed that there were only two kinds of cosmic objects: *stars* and *galaxies*. Now one seemed to be confronted with the fact that quasars constituted a *third category of cosmic objects*, heretofore totally unknown, and which therefore truly did not fit into the astronomical worldview. Compared with our solar system, a body of this sort would be extrordinarily large. Measured, on the other hand, against the size of a Milky Way it would be tiny (its diameter would amount to approximately

1/16,000,000 of the diameter of our galaxy). And here lies the problem for the second alternative, the cosmological hypothesis: *the thought of a compact body with a diameter of only several light-days which has a substantially greater mass than our Milky Way with its total of approximately 150 billion suns, to wit roughly four to ten trillion sun-masses, is something that 'explodes all physical conceptions', as one is wont to say.*

Let us consider again in what respects there is a parallel between the two examples: (1) In *both* cases the so-called facts (*on the one hand*: three received manuscripts; *on the other*: a line-spectrum) are interpreted *in the light of accepted and unquestioned background knowledge* (*on the one hand*: the poem handed down in the three manuscripts is by Walther von der Vogelweide; *on the other*: the light comes from a quasar, which is not only visible, but moreover is identical with a particular source of unimaginably strong radio waves). (2) Further appeal to background knowledge leads to a split in each case into two alternative hypotheses (*on the one hand*: the two competing interpretative hypotheses for the poem; *on the other*: the local gravitational hypothesis in contrast to the cosmological hypothesis). (3) The investigation of each alternative hypothesis leads to difficulties: *both hypotheses seem to be shaken.* We land in a *confirmation-dilemma.* (There are differences only where it is irrelevant for our problem. It is equally irrelevant that there need be no further formal parallel between the subsequent developments of the discussion in the two cases).

Is there then any difference at all? It seems to me that the difference between the two cases lies in the following: *in the natural science case we can distinguish sharply between background knowledge and facts; in the literary history case we cannot.*[8]

---

[8][This is Stegmüller's *original* conclusion, revised in what follows below (cf. for example p. 149 of this essay, and our Introduction, above, p. 38)—Eds.]

In the case from literary history we have *no sharp criterion* for distinguishing between the hypothetical components in the observational data, on the one hand, and the theoretical background knowledge on the other. In the astronomy example we can draw the boundary because the background knowledge consists of *general hypothetical laws*. In the example taken from the study of Old German literature, however, *no nontrivial laws* at all were used. It is here that the difference lies, and not in the contrast of 'mind' and 'nature', nor in the contrast between 'what one can understand' and 'what one cannot understand'—whatever this might mean more precisely.

Given the complications of the astromomy example, it would be tiresome to carry out in detail the distinction just drawn. It can be more easily illustrated in the example of *testing simple statistical hypotheses*.[9] Let us assume that two people are arguing whether a given coin has been tampered with or not. Let E be the result of observing a number *n* of coin-tosses. Let the background knowledge consist, for example, in the assumption that we are dealing with independent tosses with a probability that remains constant. (In technical terms: the background knowledge consists in the assumption that we have a binomial distribution.) This background knowledge can be recorded in a statement which we will again call the major hypothesis M. *We can of course neatly separate the two components E and M without difficulty.* For M consists of the assumption that in order to calculate the probabilities we should use the well-known statistical formula for binomial distribution; E, on the contrary, consists in a report on the result of *n* tosses of this coin.

In the historical case, and quite generally in all cases in which no use is made of hypothetical scientific laws, this tidy separation between hypothetical components among the facts and background knowledge can no longer be drawn. Let us

---

[9]For a more precise logical analysis see Stegmüller, 1973a, part III: "The logical foundations of statistical inference."

call the hypothesis under discussion in either case the "null hypothesis" (as in statistics). We can then say that in both cases the correctness of the null hypothesis is open to dispute. But it is only in the natural science example that we are able, as we are in the statistical case, to separate into two acts the attainment of agreement thanks to which the dispute makes sense: a) attaining agreement on the facts E; b) attaining agreement on the background knowledge M.

Thus, in the case from natural science we can distinguish three components: the null hypothesis H, plus M and E; in the humanities-historical case M and E flow together and we can only distinguish between H, on the one hand, and M and E, *conjoined as ME*, on the other.

What is remarkable is not that the facts are hypothetical. In *this* respect there is simply no difference between the two cases. Today there is extensive agreement that we have to surrender the naive empiricist assumption to the effect that there is something like the uninterpreted data of experience. Indeed there is nothing at all strange in this. What is remarkable is rather that in the historical case no clear boundary can be drawn between hypothetical facts and background information. Let us attempt in the Walther example to draw this boundary and to indicate precisely what *the facts* are! Do the facts consist in this, that we have before us *three pieces of writing*, i.e., copies of the three manuscripts? Or do they consist in this, that we have three documents *from circa 1300*? Or in this, that we have three copies from circa 1300 of *a poem by Walther von der Vogelweide*? Or should we also include among the facts the common opinion presupposed in discussions of this example, saying that we have here three copies of a poem by Walther von der Vogelweide, *whereby in the original e is before d*? Whichever of these alternatives we choose, the choice is *completely arbitrary*. This means no less than that every attempt to draw a boundary between the *facts* and *auxiliary background knowledge* amounts to an arbitrary choice.

Since therefore the historian, in interpreting, 'activates' no nomological knowledge at all, we can no longer speak of ready-to-hand facts being 'interpreted', in a second step, 'in the light of available background knowledge'. For *what* counts here as the observable facts only gets *determined* by the whole of that background knowledge acquired by years, even decades, of painstaking work. The reader will allow me at this point to use an image: in the facts *qua facts* the literary historian catches the 'glow' of his own background knowledge; he is unable to separate it from the hypothetical components in the factual knowledge. That is why it is also more difficult here to attain agreement about the so-called facts than it is in natural science; for the two kinds of discussions, those which lead to agreement of type a) (factual), and those which lead to agreement of type b) (background knowledge), *cannot even, in this case, be methodically separated.*

It seems to me that it is this which in fact often lies behind the thesis of the indissolubility of the so-called hermeneutic circle.

This analysis makes it *psychologically plausible* that the process of interpretation appears to the philosopher '*as a circle*': already in describing the facts '*the interpreter draws out of this description the background knowledge he smuggled into their construal*'. While in the natural scientific example there can be no question of attaining agreement about what is *seen in the spectrograph* unless there is agreement on the relevant laws of nature (e.g., agreement on the wave theory of light, the general theory of relativity, etc.), in the Walther case there can be no sharp separation between 'what is there on paper' and 'what Walther's intention was'.

I was being consciously cautious when I spoke of it being "psychologically plausible" that the method of literary critical interpretation "*appears* somehow circular." Happily it is a matter *merely of appearance*. If there were more to it, i.e., if the appearance rested on reality, it would be a logical disaster for the historical sciences: the *hermeneutical* circle would be then in truth a *vicious* circle. Happily this is not the case. And that is why the historical sciences have the same chances of survival as the nomic sciences.

In closing I would like to attempt to offer a possible explanation—one, incidentally, that is completely independent of the exposition up to this point—of the fact that the hermeneutic circle has not only occupied people's attention, but that in addition people have seen in it something like a positive distinction of the humanities. It seems to me that what Wittgenstein said about S. Freud can be paraphrased to apply to the present case (and this perhaps with even more justification than to the case Wittgenstein chose): *the theory of the hermeneutical circle has the attraction of a myth.* Its charm consists in its giving to the scientific activity of the reflective historian and philosopher *a kind of tragic pattern.* Many of us philosophers and humanities scholars will from time to time, in our work and in discussions with colleagues, have found it burdensome and unpleasant to be unable neatly to separate facts from hypotheses. And some of us, in situations in which this inseparability has become apparent in a particularly stubborn and disagreeable manner, will have harbored the secret wish, "If only I had become a natural scientist! Then I could at least say clearly, 'Here are the facts and there are the hypotheses available for explaining these facts.'" In such a frame of mind, in which we are prey to inferiority complexes with respect to the 'objective' and 'precise' natural sciences, it is perhaps a tremendous relief to be told by the hermeneuticist that in the intellectual life of a historian or a 'Verstehen'-philosopher there is something of the form of a tragedy, and that furthermore Heidegger succeeded in 'ontologically anchoring' this tragedy in the care-structure of human existence: human beings as prejudiced and repetitive beings can only extract as much understanding as they had previously invested through acts of pre-understanding.

Instead of seeking refuge in such myths we should try to achieve clarity about the real difficulties hidden behind the phrase 'circle of understanding'. As the analysis up to this point has shown, there are several heterogeneous difficulties. And as a more extensive and exact analysis will show, *all* sciences are potentially threatened by these difficulties in varying degrees.

We want now to try to make clear why this is so. At the same time I want to show why there is only a *'potential threat'*, as I just called it. What is meant is that the scientist faced with this danger need by no means capitulate to subjectivism or even irrationalism, that instead he can always, perhaps by means of a suitable alteration of his questions, both clearly formulate the problems and also discuss them in a strictly scientific framework.

The actual epistemological difficulty is not at all that one continually collides with the limits of rationality, but is rather to be seen in the fact that *various sorts* of problems overlay one another in a rather opaque manner. Once we have succeeded in distinguishing between these groups of problems, then the original task, which seemingly demanded a *global solution*, is broken down into *partial tasks*, each of which can be brought to a *particular solution*. Here we can of course only cite such solutions as are possible at the level of general epistemology. Every concrete technical discussion in which such difficulties arise must be dealt with by the appropriate specialists. This can involve, in an individual case, very considerable difficulties, as we already saw in the two case studies sketched above. In fact, *given certain limitations of knowledge*, the problems can be insoluble. But they are never insoluble *in principle*, i.e., one can in every case imagine a suitable expansion of knowledge which would lead to a solution of the difficulties. In what follows I will defend this thesis by means of an epistemological framework earmarked for the purpose.

In order not to be entangled from the start in an impenetrable thicket of questions, let us begin by making two simplifying assumptions. Both assumptions will later prove to be *fictitious*, thus basically *inadmissable* assumptions. They are nonetheless *convenient*. Their convenience will be shown in the way in which the successive liberation from them makes possible the solution of our problem and allows as well some additional, interesting insights.

As we did above, we shall here distinguish among three components of knowledge: H, the null-hypothesis under discussion; the empirical data E relevant to the evaluation of this hypothesis; and M, the background knowledge or 'major hypothesis'. The *first simplifying assumption* says: "E contains no hypothetical components at all, but is an indubitable, 'pure' experiential report." Thus we put ourselves, for the sake of experiment, back into naive empiricism, which believes in reports free of hypothetical elements. The *second simplifying assumption* says: "In the historical case, M consists solely of singular hypotheses, whereas in the case from natural science it contains only nomic hypotheses."

As clever people recognized ages ago, everything is somehow or other connected with everything else. This principle also holds for the philosophy of science. Our second assumption includes the tacit presupposition that we know what on the one hand a law is, and on the other hand a singular factual assertion. But as examples show clearly, this distinction is not such a simple affair: the singular assertion, "Socrates is a human being," can, on the Quinean pattern, be paraphrased as, "All Socratic objects are human," while the general principle, "All things are identical with themselves," can be rendered by the singular assertion, "Identity is a universal property." Some authors even feel that the question of lawlikeness is *the* problem of induction. This is in fact incorrect, for that problem is basically not philosophical at all, belonging instead to the theory of evolution. However, we can for our present purposes pretend without harm that we have a criterion at our disposal for distinguishing these two classes of statements, without us having to free ourselves in the end from this fiction, as in the case of the other two assumptions.

Let us call the distinction between statements containing reports of nonhypothetical observations and those which are hypothetical assumptions an *epistemological* distinction; and the distinction between nomic statements and those which are non-nomic a *formal* distinction. Then we can at once see that with these two assumptions the problem of the hermeneutic circle in the sense of interpretation (VI) above, disappears: *there is no longer any problem distinguishing or drawing a boundary between M and E, and that indeed in either the natural scientific or the historical case.* The reason is very simple: in the natural scientific case we can draw the boundary *purely formally,* since E consists *solely* of singular statements, while M contains *only nomic statements. In the historical case we can draw a purely epistemological* boundary, since M consists of historical assumptions, i.e., hypotheses, while E is a nonhypothetical observational report.

A side remark: given the two fictitious assumptions, there is *also* in the natural scientific case the analogous epistemological distinction between M and E as in the historical case. Thus one would have here the use of a dual criterion of distinction, one purely formal, the other epistemological.

It was already remarked above that the first simplifying assumption is untenable. Admittedly we gave no justification at that point. Both Karl Popper and Nelson Goodman, independently of one another and in quite distinct ways, have produced convincing arguments against this assumption. I do not want to rehearse those arguments here, but instead merely to point to two reasons which rest solely on the fact that we have to use *our language* for an observational report. I proceed here from Hilary Putnam's claim (in "The Meaning of 'Meaning'") that for most descriptive terms of our language—indeed for all of them except everyday expressions such as 'table', 'window', etc.—the *linguistic division of labor* holds. That is, the reference of these expressions can reliably be determined only by a small group of experts. What then does the individual competence of the nonexperts among the members of our language-community consist in, to whom of course we attribute an understanding of terms such as 'water', 'paper', 'spruce', 'orange', 'copper', 'ink', and 'lion'? The answer is: the normal speaker has associated with each of these expressions a certain *minimal standard,* which Putnam calls the *stereotype* of that expression. One could call this stereotype a 'rudimentary minitheory' of the layperson, sufficient for everyday purposes. (For example, a fir tree is stereotypically a conifer which among other things is found in the Alps; a lion is stereotypically a rather dangerous species of large cat whose adult males have a mane, etc.)

This idea goes even beyond Quine's thesis that meaning and theory cannot be neatly separated: to the extent that the everyday meaning-component consists in the stereotype, it *is* nothing else but the minitheory just mentioned.

Putnam does *not* identify the concept of meaning with the stereotype, since this would have for the philosophy of language the highly unsuitable consequence that meaning does not determine extension, but that instead there can be synonymous expressions which nonetheless differ in extension. Instead Putnam reconstucts "meaning" as a purely technical concept which has as components grammatical features, the stereotype, and also the extension. The question of the adequacy of this broader conception does not concern our present problem, and thus the simplified presentation just given is sufficient.

As should already be clear from this sketch, the stereotype—quite apart from its vagueness—can be false. On occasion the falsity even constitutes a basic trait of the normal use. A good example is the statement, "Gold is a yellow metal," which Kant and others actually regarded as analytic. It is of course correct that yellowness belongs to the stereotype of gold, provided we ignore the issue of whether to call that shining color yellow. Nonetheless, not only is this statement not analytic, it is instead false. For pure or paradigmatic gold is never yellow, but white. (The yellowness comes from an admixture of copper, about which the everyday person ordinarily knows nothing.) Incidentally, it here becomes clear how closely connected the linguistic division of labor is with the economic divison of labor. For the 'nonexperts' who have a lot to do with gold are jewelers and jewelry dealers, presidents of central banks, makers of monetary policy, as well as people who fear inflation; and all of these usually see only 'yellow gold'. *The human-fallible component which threatens every stereotype rules out our ever being able to employ the corresponding expressions to make absolutely certain statements*.[10]

[10]Expert knowledge is, by the way, also threatened by 'fallibilism'. This too can be not only occasionally mistaken, it can be permanently

There is also a second point. I used the phrase that the stereotype is "associated with the expression." This too should not be interpreted to mean that an *indissoluble* linkage has been established here. 'Memory illusions' can also affect just this linkage of word and stereotype. If I have acquired today an understanding of the words 'gold' and 'silver', I have nonetheless no guarantee that tomorrow I shall not connect the gold stereotype with 'silver' and the silver stereotype with 'gold'.

Let us return to our point of departure. The digression was only meant to convince us quickly that the first simplifying assumption is incorrect. There is no getting around the concession that, as do H and M, E also contains hypothetical components. It should be added that these components constitute an *indefinite* totality which we are incapable of specifying, about which indeed we are not capable of providing ourselves a systematic overview. If we wanted to do this, we would need to be able to reconstruct the development of language and of 'thinking', i.e., a process lasting many hundreds of millions of years, and this of course is ruled out. We only become aware of the fact that there is something hypothetical in an E when we find *reasons to doubt* our so-called empirical reports and even more in those cases in which, having been led by our doubts to investigate further, we are forced to declare the original report mistaken.

One can understand this assertion about E, which is nowadays hardly in dispute, as the weakest form of the *thesis of the theory-ladenness of observations*. How does the problem of the hermeneutical circle present itself, given this assumption? Let us try to give a short systematic comparison of the two case studies. It will be useful for us to distinguish, thereby following Aristotle, between the level of the objective contexts (briefly, the *objective* aspect) and the level of the *epistemic* contexts, the aspect under which it presents itself 'for us'

'false'. Compare here Putnam's critical discussion of Wilson's principle of charity, in "Language and Reality," Putnam, 1975.

(briefly, the *epistemological* aspect). In each case *what is for us prior*—the 'observational fact'—*is objectively later*, since the facts 'presented' to us represent the *effects* visible today of processes which are either long past or else are happening in far removed areas of the universe. The expressions 'primary' and 'secondary' are chosen in accord with the epistemological contexts, not the objective contexts. The primary facts T1 are in the one case the various received versions of Walther's poem (74,20) here before us on the table; in the other case they consist in what shows itself in the spectroscope aimed at quasar 3C 273. From T1 we want to infer T2, the secondary fact. In the one case this is Walther's 'true poem', in the other case it is the 'true nature' of the quasar. The null-hypothesis H, whether sought after or in need of confirmation, serves to describe this secondary fact.

Let us first pursue the situation for the natural scientific case. We assume we can distinguish sharply between E and M. This assumption, however, immediately proves to be dubious. For, although E describes in this case the observations in the spectroscope, it includes, among other hypothetical components, especially the following: first, a theory of the measuring apparatus, including all the physical presuppositons contained in the theory; secondly, the assumption that this instrument in front of me is 'functioning correctly'. But the first is nomic knowledge, so that someone might immediately object, "You are thereby already appealing to background knowledge!" Let us completely concede this point to the objector. We simply resolve, however, *not* to regard the knowledge here employed as a constituent of M, but rather to remove it from M.[11] I want to call it *entrance knowledge*, because it already gains access to the interpretation of the observational report, i.e., is already used for the description

[11]Speculation about whether this procedure is sensible, feasible, or even possible can be omitted here, since it is only a matter of a provisional distinction for the sake of clarification, one which we shall later discard.

of T1. In the present case the entrance knowledge leads us to the finding that a huge red-shift is observed. Thus this knowledge should be a constituent of E.

To M, on the other hand, we should reckon all and only those elements which we need, as one says, 'to infer T2'. (This talk of 'inferring' is, speaking strictly logically, a metaphor, since what is supposed to be inferred here is precisely the hypothesis H, for which, at most, supporting data can be given.) Since it is a matter of *evaluating* E, we will mark off the background knowledge M from the entrance knowledge by use of the term '*evaluation knowledge*'. Thus the evaluation knowledge is *called in* only "after there is no longer any reasonable doubt about the available observations."

The attempt to evaluate E leads in this first step only to a *bifurcation*. The '*bifurcation knowledge*' utilized in the process can be formulated roughly like this: "According to all we know about light, a red-shift can only be attributed either to the Doppler effect or else to the fact that the light has to struggle with an immense gravitational field."

For the further evaluation of each case an appeal is now made to a *second-step knowledge*, coming thereby closer to the two *possible* secondary states of affairs. The first alternative leads to the neutron-star hypothesis with the physical 'impossibilities' mentioned earlier. The second alternative leads to one of the contemporary quasar hypotheses, together with all the attendant (temporary?) difficulties. What sort of available knowledge enters in here? In any case, quite an extraordinary amount: in the first case, the general theory of relativity as well as a good deal of what we know of 'the theory of neutron stars'. In the second case—even if one is chary of further astrophysical speculation—at least the wave theory of light, the theory of the Doppler effect, and the hypothesis of the limit-character of the speed of light.

An aside: there is an asymmetry between these two cases which rules out a perfect analogy to the historical case. To the two *interpretative hypotheses* in the latter case, competing *explanatory hypotheses* would correspond. We possess that kind of explanatory model only in the case of the local gravitational hypothesis, i.e., the supernova theory. So far no one has found a convincing, generally accepted model for the cosmological hypothesis. Is it a question, as I suspect, of protogalactic processes? Are we dealing with the highly active centers of radio galaxies? Is it perhaps really a different class of cosmic 'object-processes' which no longer exist, since all the quasars have in the meantime 'burned out'?

What we need to hold on to for the sake of comparison with the other case study is a simple result. Once we have gotten straight, on the one hand, what sort of already available knowledge *goes into E*, and, on the other hand, what sort of information is *called in after E* is fixed, then not only can we achieve a clear view of the situation, but it will also never happen to us that the two 'levels of facts' T1 and T2 fuse together. We shall always be able to distinguish sharply between the processes 'there before us in the spectroscope' and the 'quasars out there in space'.

Does this hold equally for the historical case? I shall begin by first confronting an objection often encountered but which nonetheless rests on a basic misunderstanding. This is the contention that the studies by Wapnewski and Hahn should be viewed as 'out-of-date', unsuitable for an up-to-date discussion. One has to reply that this is simply a confusion of the tasks of a Germanist with those of a philosopher of science. This can be illustrated most simply with the concept of the case study: Walther's poem would constitute a case study in German literary criticism. *That is not our case study*! The philosophical example consists *in the dispute between the two Germanists about Walther's poem.* It would of course be essential for an up-to-date discussion of German literature to take heed as well of other results, especially *those achieved with different scholarly methods.* We could also include this sort of thing in our philosophical considerations, but to no gain at all; we would rather have increased the danger that "we have first raised a dust, and then complain, we cannot see," to quote Bishop Berkeley. It is always useful for philosophical analyses first to look for the simplest and most easily grasped examples, shifting to more complicated ones only if simple ones cannot be found. We have no need of such a shift, as will to some extent still be shown.

The situation of the quasar example is by the way no different: I have depicted an alternative there which is meant to analogize the historical example *as completely as possible.* It would be out of place to start a technical scientific discussion about it. The depiction above is not suitable even as a starting point for such a discussion. If an astrophysicist *today* would begin with the depicted alternative, he would of course seem simply ridiculous to his colleagues.

Let us now return to our historical case study. For the sake of simplicity we will assume that the three versions of the poem in the original form are before me on the table. We have no need to go back further, say to so-called 'sense-data', since we have already freed ourselves of the first simplifying assumption. Furthermore the sense-data theory was only *one* vain attempt to purify the observational report E of all hypothetical components. It would on the other hand be perfectly permissable to raise, e.g., the question whether we are really dealing here with *human* handwriting or whether the ostensible writing could have gotten onto the paper by accident. It is true that every historian and Germanist will presuppose a negative answer as a matter of course. The rationale, however, would be the province of an expert in statistical inference. As one can see, the scientific division of labor potentially takes hold rather early here too.

We want to leave it to the reader to think out how the scholar pondering this poem comes successively, in the course of his investigations and reflections, to add to E more and more of his background knowledge M, material either available to him from the start or else gradually expanded through consultation of other experts. Put in our earlier terminology, what originally seemed aimed at serving as 'evaluation knowledge', to be *called in subsequently* to increase our understanding of what was made available in E, instead gets used as 'entrance knowledge' in E and is taken *as a constituent of the empirical finding itself.* The result is something highly peculiar: not only does the boundary between E and M become fluid, the tripartite division of E, M, and H (where H is, say, the conjunction of H3 and H4) collapses completely. *In the end E, sufficiently enriched by elements of the background knowledge, contains H itself as a component*!

How is such a thing possible? Or is there not some logical error here after all? The empirical report, one wants to counter, cannot after all swallow up, so to speak, the hypothesis under discussion! But that is exactly what happens. And that is also what constitutes the psychologically so peculiar state of affairs known as the hermeneutical circle. It is also obvious that we hereby land in a *confirmation-dilemma*: the observational reports in E are indeed supposed to represent precisely an *independent* tribunal for judging and testing the hypothesis H. If however this hypothesis now melts inextricably into the data, how should a test still be possible at all? We have thus formulated the problem in terms of interpretation (V).

Let us for the moment try to analyze our intermediate result more precisely. This is how things stand: not only can we not clearly mark off the hypothetical components in E from those in M, we also cannot simply shift the deductive and inductive 'patterns of inference' into the one or the other area. For there will always be some inferences or other, either more primitive or more complicated. In particular, everything that serves as entrance knowledge must enter into inferences in order to be able to lead to interpretation of E. Thus we cannot mark off the background information by saying of it, for example, that it is the knowledge which serves as premises in deductive inferences or as data for 'inductive confirmatory inferences'. But that would make it admissible to take all the necessary background knowledge as *'entrance knowledge' for E*. That this in the end also includes the hypothesis H is due simply to the facts that, first of all, a sufficiently rich portion of M implies this H, and, secondly, just such an adequately strong part of M has been utilized as entrance knowledge for E. Using the language of the two categories of facts, this means that, while the primary fact T1, consisting of the three texts here before me, could at first be clearly distinguished from the 'inferred' secondary fact T2, consisting of the poem composed by Walther 700 years ago, in the course of the research mentioned the boundary between the two begins to blur as T2 gradually becomes part of T1. Thus it was not merely a metaphor, but rather meant quite seriously, when I said before *that no sharp boundary exists between 'what is there on paper' and 'what Walther's intention was'*. In any case it is no wonder if the specialist who has perhaps devoted years to the study, direct or indirect (sources, cultural comparison, etc.), of the material finally comes to feel that his hypothesis H is no hypothesis at all, that he instead extracts from the data only 'what he knew right along'. Leaving this 'right along' to one side, he has quite correctly described his impression.

This of course does nothing to alter the fact that we are not faced here with a logical circle; we can discuss H in a perfectly rational manner. For this to be possible, the 'seepage from M into E' has to be reversed to the point where E contains only hypotheses admitted by both discussants, while everything else 'slips back' into the once again problematical background knowledge. In the process the hypothesis H, which had previously been 'swallowed up by E', once again becomes visible *as such*.

This is not to assert that it is easy to reverse the inclusion of background knowledge in the entrance knowledge utilized to interpret the observational finding. It may prove difficult for the individual scholar to question things which for him have long since become more or less obvious 'facts'. Frequently he will not even be aware that there is anything at all problematical about his interpretive assumptions until he encounters the contrary opinion of some fellow scholar. What can he do in this case? Let us assume that he appeals to background knowledge M1, his colleague to M2. At first both must try to retreat to what (one hopes!) is the non-empty intersection of M1 and M2, i.e., their common convictions. The simplest case of further development is that consisting solely of a *simple exchange of information*: each provides the other with additional information which the other did not yet have, and which, once he has acquired it, he no longer doubts. In these ideal circumstances they will be able in the end to cooperate further on the richer foundation of the union of M1 and M2. Even this rare ideal case does not guarantee final agreement on the hypothesis under discussion, to the extent that this hypothesis does not follow logically from their common knowledge. They can have differing opinions about the 'degree of support' of this hypothesis.

If such is the case, then in all likelihood the disagreement will become obvious even earlier. And then it can indeed happen that a *philosophical* discussion about the support and about the circumstances under which a hypothesis is to be accepted or rejected might facilitate agreement. But something like an *incommensurability* might also be the result. The one might be a cautious sort 'who refuses to stray from the practically undeniable facts', the other however a thinker who takes satisfaction only in putting forward 'bold' hypotheses. There is nothing logically disquieting about this sort of 'incommensurability', however uncongenial it may be for those involved. It is an incommensurability, not of the facts described or of the theories accepted, but of *character*. Similarly, the difference between 'skeptics' and 'nonskeptics' frequently (or even mostly) does not reflect any difference in views, but rather only an incompatibility of character dispositions.

Where opinions clash strongly, however, it seems that normally neither this sort of "incommensurability of character" nor an epistemologically specifiable "difference of supporting and test theories" is at issue. Rather, it will prove mostly to involve a *difference of opinion specific to that discipline over which methodology to apply*. There is indeed no objection to calling this too a *philosophical* difference of opinion. However we should then sharply distinguish between general and specific philosophy of science, assigning the above-mentioned second possible reason for a difference of opinion to the former, and the reason just mentioned to the latter. As long as there is no developed "philosophy of science for German literary studies," what I just called the difference of opinion specific to the discipline will have to be carried out among Germanists.

I must here make do with these suggestions, since we still have to turn to several more fundamental questions, the first of which is this: *to what extent is that which is apparently illustrated by the two case studies*—the sharp separability of E and M in the one case, their inseparability in the other—*paradigmatic for particular branches of science*? It would seem that what we have said up to this point already answers this question, but such an assumption would rest on an error.

We need now to remind ourselves that in the entire discussion up to now we freed ourselves from the first simplified assumption, but not from the second. It will now become at once apparent that I must again revise many statements in which *ostensible* interim results were recorded. *It is no less incorrect to assume that the background knowledge of the historian contains only singular hypotheses, while that of the natural scientist contains only hypothetical laws, than it was to make the first simplifying assumption.*

Let us begin with the example from natural science. It would, to be sure, be inadmissable to bring against the second simplifying assumption the assertion that the natural scientist must presuppose as valid the hypothesis, "This spectroscope functions correctly." For this kind of assumption belongs to the *entrance knowledge* that has become a component of E. Should M contain only hypothetical laws, the sharp separability of E and M in principle would remain conceivable.

Why this is nonetheless not so can best be seen if one considers the arguments for the conclusions which follow from the local gravitation hypothesis. I spoke of this quite vaguely as the "hypothesis of neutron stars." How does it happen that today's astronomers know rather a lot about these entities, in particular also about their pre-history and formation? To a large extent they know these things thanks to a *happy historical coincidence*, to wit the explosion of a supernova about 900 years ago (in 1054) at the relatively close distance of 'only' a thousand light-years from us. This explosion was carefully observed by Chinese astronomers. Since their specifications of location were also quite precise, we know that this event must have taken place in the so called "Crab Nebula," in the interior of which a pulsar was discovered. This was the best confirmation for the assumption that pulsars are neutron stars, predicted by the theory and long sought-for, left as residual stars after a supernova explosion. The Crab Nebula, which originated in 1054 and has since attained an extension of several light-years, consists of that portion of the matter which was at the time hurled out into space.

So it was the precise scientific investigations *of a quite definite, individual 'historical' object,*[12] this Crab Nebula and the pulsar contained within it, which provided support for the theory in question. If only for that reason, there can be no talk of the astrophysicist in our model case appealing *only to law-like* statements in this background knowledge.

It is, on the other hand, no less false to say that the historian makes no use of nomic knowledge. Not even Popper's conjecture that such knowledge is always *trivial* in historical cases need be correct.[13] If in the case of the poem (74,20) the suspicion should arise that the supposed manuscripts from circa 1300 in reality were *forgeries from some later century,* complicated physico-chemical analyzes of the paper and ink used could become necessary to settle the dispute. Frequently statements of a third kind, neither singular (in a sense) nor nomic (in a sense), are used. One could characterize them as *statements of cultural regularities.* Should, for example, the above mentioned physico-chemical results allow no reliable inferences, the dispute would indeed thereby have been returned to the "humanities sphere," but that does not mean that one would have to rely solely on knowledge about

---

[12]With respect to the predicate 'historical' one should recall that what we see today in the Crab Nebula happened some 1000 years ago. The explosion of the supernova should be correspondingly back-dated. With the phrase, "This explosion was observed in 1054," we of course refer to an event on *our planet,* to wit the observations of the aforesaid Chinese astronomers.

[13]I am grateful to Professor K. Hübner of Kiel for pointing this out to me.

special objects. In addition one could and would fall back on knowledge about *general cultural regularities* concerning the script and writing style of the time, as well as the use of particular types of paper common in that age.

Thus the response to the above question is *purely negative*. More precisely: *if and to the extent that one understands the phenomenon of the hermeneutical circle in the manner of interpretations (V), and (VI), then no justification can be given for distinguishing between, say, the humanities and natural sciences, or historical and nomic sciences*. We have thereby belatedly verified the earlier thesis that potentially *all* sciences are threatened by the aforesaid difficulties.

It may serve as a further illustration if we bring home by use of the astrophysical example why it would be illusory here too to draw a sharp demarcation between a) the *entrance knowledge* used in interpreting the observational findings, and b) the *background knowledge called upon to evaluate these findings* once they are *available*. Were we to present our alternative to an experienced astronomer, that person would, in a fraction of a second, 'mentally review' the reasons which speak against the local gravitiation hypothesis and assert something like this: "The correct interpretation of observational finding E shows that Quasar 3C 273 must be more than 6000 light years away." A great deal of what, in our original description of the situation, belonged to the '*evaluation knowledge' summoned up subsequently* is treated by this astronomer as '*entrance knowledge' serving the interpretation of E*.

A further important question is connected with the theme of the 'theory-ladenness of observation'. Confronted with our thesis that an observational finding E is never unequivocal, i.e., the boundary between E and M is subject to a *general variability*, one is tempted by the manifest objection *that the concepts of observation and observational finding are being used irresponsibly here*. A similar reproach has been made against the various versions of the thesis that one's perceptions and observations are always partly determined by the theories one holds. Even Quine, who because of his holism and his retreat from the 'dogmas of empiricism' represents a very liberal form of empiricism, accuses philosophers such as M. Polanyi, T. S. Kuhn and N. R. Hanson of 'epistemological nihilism' because their views 'restrict the role of observation' and 'stress cultural relativism.'[14] Can a similar reproach be made against the view put forward here?

Considerations of space rule out a detailed analysis here, so I shall limit myself to one remark and one graphic analogy. Not only do we not limit the role of observation as an 'intersubjective tribunal' for the evaluation of hypotheses when we discover hypothetical components in all observational reports; we limit it no less when we declare the boundary between *these* hypotheses and *those belonging to the background knowledge* to be variable in the sense of being *relativized to a given treatment of some problem*. If the former constitutes no objection to speaking of findings, neither does the latter. For the variability holds *for both parts*. Just as any given empirical datum E can be successively *enriched* if one keeps adding to it elements of the background knowledge—our catchphrase: '*available evaluation knowledge becomes entrance knowledge*'—so conversely can each such hypothetical component be removed again from E and relegated to the background knowledge, whether it be to subject it to critical scrutiny, or merely to make the finding look scantier, to be sure, but thereby all the more reliable. To use an analogy from the synthesis of proteins, just as the ribosomes form the *firm foundation* on which the amino acids are knitted together into peptide chains, the observations form the firm foundation for a process which here, however, can potentially unfold in both directions: it can 'flow into' E, or 'flow out' into M. It is always a matter of more or less interpretation of the *observations*.

Quine's criticism was, to be sure, aimed at something different, i.e., against a view characterized by slogans such as "Theories create their own facts." These difficulties belong to

[14] W. V. O. Quine, 1969, pp. 87f.

the *theoretical circle*, topic (III), which has been dealt with elsewhere in depth[15] and about which I will here make a few brief remarks. What are 'facts for a theory'? Let us assume that the theory in question is classical particle mechanics (CP). The applications of this theory consist of systems of particles; each is endowed with mass, and forces operate among them. A 'fact' is described by a correct statement about the particles *thus endowed.* To test this statement we must among other things determine the values of the force function. In the course of carrying out this determination we encounter a fundamental difficulty: every procedure for measuring forces presupposes the validity of the laws of classical particle mechanics, to wit the validity of Newton's Second Law as well as a further special law of force. Sneed expressed the matter like this: *the values of the force function are measured in a theory-dependent manner.* If I want to test whether *one* application of CP is successful, I must presuppose that *another* application of CP was successful. This time we do land in a *genuine logical circle.*[16]

We can call this *the problem of theoretical terms*, and it applies to the two CP-theoretical terms *force* and *mass*. How does one get out of this difficulty? Answer: one must take a step back and refer to kinematic systems alone. Then the empirical assertions of CP say that such systems, *supplemented* in the appropriate manner by functions, are *models of CP.* 'Realist' talk about forces and masses is thus replaced by certain existential assertions. This is the so-called *Ramsey-solution to the problem of theoretical terms.*[17] To this day it re-

---

[15]Compare J. D. Sneed, 1971, pp. 38ff.; and W. Stegmüller, 1976, pp. 63ff. Because of the many misunderstandings of the criterion of theoreticity I have once again discussed it, this time in more detail, in my 1979, section 4.

[16]More precisely: if the number of applications of the theory is finite, we land in a circle. If the number is not finite, we land either in a circle or in an infinite regress.

[17]It should be mentioned in passing that this last difficulty and its solution can be utilized both to make more precise and to support

mains unknown whether there are other possible solutions to this difficulty.

I had to mention this problem at least once more. For wherever it turns up, this difficulty superimposes itself upon the questions with which I have mainly been concerned here, i.e., problems V and VI. This superimposition of the problems can indeed on occasion lead to an unpleasant and rather impenetrable situation, though not to a task that is insoluble in principle.

Summary

The phrase 'circle of understanding' proved to apply to an entire conceptual family of problems. These problems are *genuine* difficulties, and not *pseudo-problems*, as antihermeneuticists occasionally claim. Each individual member of this family can be dealt with in a precise analytical manner. We cannot, it is true, give a 'philosophical global solution' wherever one of these difficulties appears; for to find the solution is always the business of the specialists in each discipline. What we were able to show was that such solutions always exist in principle.

Further, we saw that certain forms of the circle of understanding are closely connected to the 'problem of the theory-ladenness of observation.'

And finally we have come to see that no form of this circle at all can be used systematically to demarcate, much less 'to indicate the special feature' of, the humanities or historical sciences vis-à-vis the natural or nonhistorical sciences. For, to stress this point once more, every branch of science is potentially threatened by all these difficulties.

Feyerabend's thesis of the *theory-dependence of the meaning of theoretical terms*; compare my 1976, p. 277.

4

Literary-Critical Interpretation—Psychoanalytic Interpretation

Ernst Konrad Specht

In the contemporary dispute over the scientific status of psychoanalysis the issue of what, logically, an interpretation is has thus far been insufficiently clarified. Our everyday concept of interpretation is quite broad and covers such varied items as the interpretation of an oracle, the Einsteinian interpretation of the perihelion of Mercury, Rorschach interpretations, the Marxian interpretation of the Eighteenth Brumaire, etc. Now to which type are we to assign psychoanalytic interpretations? Can they be compared with certain interpretations occasionally given in the natural sciences? Think for instance of the following example: in America fossilized human footprints were found in the surface strata of Carboniferous rock. This discovery of course contradicts all the paleontological notions of the first appearance of human beings.[1] There are two *interpretations* of these peculiar prints.

The first interpretation comes from certain Presbyterian congregations which hold to a literal understanding of Genesis and hence believe in the Flood as a historical event. These

[1]I take this example from Erben, 1975, pp. 169 ff., a book which is philosophically instructive in other respects too.

Presbyterians interpret the prints as genuine footprints of those who left Noah's Ark and stepped into the mud left behind by the Flood.

The second interpretation comes from the geologists who discovered these prints. They explain them as artificial creations cut into the stone by prehistoric Indians. For the Indians regarded the human foot as a mythological symbol, and thus depicted it again and again.

But why, in the case of this geological explanation, do we not speak simply of an 'explanation', saying instead that the geologists *interpreted* the footprints thus and so? In my opinion two marks are here decisive which at the same time may be assumed to be characteristic of all interpretations:

a) We give an interpretation when the explanandum in question (a fossil, a text, a historical event) admits several explanations (in the broadest sense of the term), without our being able conclusively to verify or falsify one of the explanations (either temporarily or in principle). Thus, for example, an oracle is 'equivocal', i.e., it always admits several explanations of what the god meant with the utterance, without our being able really to grasp the god's intention. Similarly, the footprints in the Carboniferous rock are 'not univocal', since, that is, they are so weathered that we can no longer recognize possible chisel-marks.[2]

b) The second element of an interpretation consists in its containing a subjective stipulation, i.e., considering the lack of objective decision-procedures, it represents a subjective decision in favor of one of the possible explanations of the phenomenon.

True, the geologists cannot objectively establish their explanation of the footprints; but the arguments which speak for

---

[2]It should be mentioned that there are undoubted fossilized footprints of human beings, to wit those in ice age caves in France. One of these prints had become filled with limestone sinter and permitted recognition of the finest details of the skin on the human foot. In a case like this "there is nothing to interpret." On this point cf. Erben again, p.457.

this explanation and against that of the Presbyterians are so convincing for the geologists that they decide in favor of accepting their own conception and stipulate it as correct.

It becomes apparent, by the way, that in spite of the subjective element in the formation of an interpretation, arguments and reasoning play by all means a weighty role; interpretations are not supposed to be subjective phantasies. Even in the interpretation of oracles there are definite, though not highly canonized rules in accordance with which one has to proceed; and such an interpretation occasionally attains the level of the highest rationality: compare the interpretation of his famous oracle given by Socrates in the *Apology*.[3]

Now in logical terms the geologists' interpretation has the status of a *hypothesis*, understanding here by 'hypothesis' a proposition which is asserted as true and can in principle be clearly verified or falsified. One can easily imagine that sooner or later paleontology will have access to further data or methods of investigation by means of which the interpretation of the footprints can be clearly proved.

To the extent that interpretations are hypotheses, they have a provisional character. They actually represent a temporary expedient for want of sufficient information and are in principle replaceable by something better, to wit by a demonstrated proposition.

Now one might initially suppose that the overlapping of interpretation and hypothesis which here becomes manifest is a general mark of all interpretations. But this is not the case: there are interpretations which are not hypotheses, as we will now make clear with the example of a literary critical interpretation. We choose for this purpose the interpretation of a poem by Stefan George:

Anniversary

O sister, take the gray earthen jug,
Accompany me! for you have not forgotten

[3]Plato, *Apology*, 20e 6.

The pious ritual custom we have kept.
Today it is seven summers since we heard,
As we talked while drawing water from the well:
On the same day our bridegroom died.
Let us, at the spring where two poplars
Stand with a pine in the meadows,
Fetch water in the gray earthen jug.[4]

This poem is, in all its brevity, extraordinarily cryptic and raises many hermeneutical questions; we shall restrict ourselves to asking how many persons are mentioned in this poem, and how the relationship between them is to be understood. Morwitz (1960), for example, asserted that four persons are spoken of, two women who were engaged to two different men. The two women learn on a particular day that their respective fiancés died at the same time. Each year the two women commemorate this day as the beginning of a sisterly friendship based on their common mourning for the deceased fiancés.[5]

To be sure, misgivings about this interpretation arise at once. In the final three lines of the poem there is strikingly precise mention of *two* poplars and *one* pine; if we want to integrate this nature image, with its precise numerical detail, into the human events of the poem (say, in the manner of an

---

[4]From Stefan George, 1966. [A selection of these poems, including "Anniversary" ("Jahrestag") has been translated by Ernst Morwitz and Carol North Valhope, in Morwitz, 1943. Strikingly, the translation follows Morwitz's own interpretation of the poem, discussed below by Specht, even to the extent of translating the German singular *bräutigam* (*sic*) of the original by the English plural, "bridegrooms." The Morwitz-Valhope translation, unlike our own literal rendition here, is itself a poem of considerable beauty.—Eds.]

[5]"Seven years ago, as both (women) were fetching water at the well on a particular day, they had learned that their fiancés had died at the same time. Ever since they had gone to the well together at the yearly return of that day, once again to fetch water, and this walk had become for them a memorial rite." Morwitz, 1960, pp. 57 f.

Ovidian metamorphosis), we can in fact relate it only to three persons.

Accordingly, Bock (1957) produced a divergent interpretation from that of Morwitz: the poem tells of two women who—without knowing it—loved one and the same man. On a particular day they learn at the same time that their beloved has died, and they thereby discover that they loved one and the same man. The two women commemorate this day of knowledge as the start of a sisterly friendship. In this manner Bock can easily refer the nature image of the three trees to the three personages of the poem.

Admittedly this interpretation also faces a particular difficulty: 'bridegroom' ordinarily means a man who has given a woman a more or less official pledge (and this man on the day of the wedding!). Thus if one takes the word in its ordinary meaning, then the deceased man must have been betrothed twice. Bock attempts to avoid this consequence by re-interpreting the word 'bridegroom' as 'beloved', the one the women 'had elected as bridegroom'. This meaning is especially familiar to us in conjunction with the bridal estate of nuns, who have elected Christ as bridegroom.[6]

If, however, one is unwilling to go along with this re-interpretation, holding on instead to the ordinary meaning of 'bridegroom', then the result is a third interpretation. According to this one the poem would indeed refer to two women and one man, but, in contrast to Bock's interpetation, this man would have become engaged to both women. One day the women learn that their bridegroom died on the same day, which reveals to them the painful fact that they had both been deceived and cheated by him. The women commemo-

[6]"For we are not confronted with two brides and two bridegrooms at all, but rather two girls who loved one and the same shepherd, had elected him and no one else as bridegroom. Now we become aware of the reason why the sisters today want to go to 'the' spring, the one which is *their* spring, because there '*two* poplars stand with *one* pine in the meadows.'" Bock, 1957, pp. 18–19.

rate this day of loss and bitter disappointment as the start of a sisterly friendship.[6a]

This interpretation would see the origin of the sisterly relationship between the two women not so much in shared sorrow as in shared disappointment about the man, with the addition of a special emotional quality from the fact that the women now bound to one another in this sisterly way would actually be competitors had their beloved not died. One could of course object to this interpretation by contending that it does not fit with a certain 'lofty' tone which some interpreters claimed to find in the *Hirtengedichte* (*Eclogues*), i.e., a general mood of the sort which Hofmannsthal, for example, described in his discussion of the first private edition: "Something sublimely human, in which the reader can share without reservation."[7] In the train of this argumentation against the third interpretation one could also refer to the fact that in the poem the phrase "pious ritual custom" is used: such an epithet would fit the remembrance of a departed loved one, but hardly the case history of a fraudulent bridegroom.

We have now presented three interpretations of George's poem and would naturally like to know which is the *correct* interpretation. First of all, in the spirit of a correspondence theory of truth one would say that the correct interpretation is the one which agrees with the author's intention, with what the author means with the text. Now in interpreting a poem one can of course make it one's goal to grasp the intention of the author, and this is indeed often enough the goal of a literary critical interpretation.

Goethe's "Harzreise im Winter" ("Winter Journey through the Harz Mountains") ends with the well-known apostrophe of the Brocken Peak:

[6a]See Schulz, 1967, p. 14.

[7]Hofmannsthal, 1956, I, pp. 282 f.: "The controlled grace of ancient statues of boys . . . bashfulness and modest arrogance . . . a youthful, half-sensual piety . . . but the infinitely high seriousness of youth . . . "

You tower, your unfathomed bosom
Mysteriously manifest,
O'er the astonished world,
And peer down from the clouds
Across its realms and splendour,
Which you water from the veins of your brothers
Beside you.

Since Goethe, on his Harz journey at the end of November 1777, visited—among others—the mining operations at Illmenau, one could interpret "veins of your brothers" as the author's allusion to the veins of metal in the mountains around the Brocken Peak. In point of fact this interpretation can be verified with the help of Goethe's own utterance from the year 1821 in which he comments on this passage: "There is here a quiet allusion to the mining operations. The unfathomed bosom of the main peak is opposed to the veins of its brothers. The veins of metal are meant, from which the realms of the world and their splendour are watered."[8]

Interpretations which aim in this manner at the author's intention have the logical status of a hypothesis verifiable in principle. To this extent they thoroughly resemble the (hypothetical) interpretation of the geologists.

But many literary critical interpretations aim precisely not at the author's intention, so that the correctness of the interpretation in these cases cannot consist in a correspondence of interpretation and author's intention. This is especially so when authors themselves do not claim for their own intentions the status of the exclusive and true sense of their texts.

But this is precisely the case with George, who declared that a reader might wrest from his poems a (legitimate) sense which he himself had not thought of.[9] Thus in the case of our

[8]Goethe, 1967, I, p. 311; II, p. 597. Of course such a verification is valid only when the author is not subject to deceptive memory. Caution is always appropriate. In the present case, e.g., Goethe confused the dates. He dated the journey at the end of November 1776. But it actually took place at the end of November 1777.

[9]"George wanted interpretation, he taught the young friends to give a literal account, strictly according to grammar and punctuation. He

poem the author's intention certainly cannot be used as the final and absolute court of verification.

In these circumstances can we still speak of a 'correct' interpretation at all? Certainly not in terms of the correspondence theory of truth. Neither the author's intention nor the text so determine the sense of the George poem that we could give this sense in a true proposition.[10] The interpretation of the poem consists rather in one *deciding* to accept one of the possible readings, thereby clearly fixing the sense of the text only in the act of interpretation. Let us call interpretations which in this manner determine the sense of the text through subjective construal 'constructive interpretations.'

Now we had seen that the element of subjective postulation plays an essential role in all interpretations. What is special about constructive interpretations is simply that in their case no preliminary, subjective hypothesis is advanced about a sense that is itself clear-cut and which could someday be objectively confirmed. Instead it is only in a subjective act of decision that the sense of the poem gets stipulated, constructed, 'founded' at all. For this reason constructive interpretations are indeed not stopgaps, replaceable someday by a proven assertion.

But this is of course not to say that in constructive interpretations the door is opened for subjective license—as is largely the case with the interpretation of oracles and as is

---

gave the the poems the right to stand for themselves; he could perhaps find another meaning of which he was not conscious as he wrote the poem; indeed later readers might perhaps succeed at this." Hildebrandt, 1961, p. 359.

[10]Of course not all statements about the meaning of a text are interpretations. There are indeed statements about text passages which are correct beyond doubt. Effi Briest, e.g., writes from Munich during her honeymoon: "Dear Mama, Visited the Pinakothek this morning. Geert wanted to go over the other one too, which I will not name here since I am in doubt about the spelling and don't want to ask him." There can be no doubt that the Glyptothek is meant here, and not, say, the Frauenkirche or the Propylaen. Cf. Th. Fontane, *Effi Briest*, chap. 5.

frankly meant to be triggered in Rorschach interpretations. We have indeed presented three different interpretations of the poem, none of which is entirely off the point;[11] but we have also extensively substantiated each individual interpretation with arguments and counterarguments.

The first interpretation (two women, engaged to two different men) is faced, for example, with the difficulty of being unable to integrate the nature image of the three trees.

The second interpretation (two women, each of whom has elected the same man as bridegroom) can explain the nature image; it has a problem however with the word 'bridegroom'. The third interpretation (two women, one man who has become engaged to both of them) is superior to the other two to the extent that it can explain the nature image and does not need to reinterpret 'bridegroom'. To be sure one can oppose to this interpretation the charge that it is out of harmony with the mood of the 'sublimely human', thus encountering difficulties with the expression "pious ritual custom."

Looking over these arguments we see now that we can with their help surely exclude a multitude of absurd, artificial, off-the-point interpretations; but the arguments nevertheless do not suffice to reach an 'objective' decision among the three readings. Thus in this situation we are forced to consider and weigh the grounds for ourselves and then to make a subjective decision to accept one of the interpretations.

I, for example, am personally inclined to decide in favor of the third interpretation. Compared with the other two it has the advantage of being able to explain the nature image while not having to reinterpret the word 'bridegroom'. The counterargument (that this interpretation fails to correspond to the basic mood of the collection of poems) seems to me none too weighty in the light of the fact that there is a series of passages which do not at all fit to the "sublimely human."[12] As for the

[11]An example of an incorrect interpretation would be, for example, the assertion that the two poplars and the one pine are to be understood as an allusion to Christ, Mary, and Mary Magdalen.

[12]Cf., for example, the bloody suicide-threat in the poem "Dialog in the Reeds": "This knife (you see it) with which I peel the sap-filled

"pious ritual custom," one must point out that with their yearly walk to the spring the two women commemorate, not the man's day of death, but instead the anniversary of the start of their sisterly relationship (as Bock too, 1957, p. 19, called to our attention). Thus all three interpretations are faced with the question why the two women commemorate the start of their friendship in the form of an almost religious ritual, in a "pious ritual custom," and therefore one cannot use this argument specifically against the third interpretation.

These considerations make it very clear once again how argument and subjective decision combine in literary critical interpretation. It also becomes clear, I think, why constructive interpretations are not hypotheses in principle capable of being verified. Constructive interpretations simply have a quite different logical status from hypotheses, and they represent the only appropriate form for explaining the sense of a text which is not univocal and whose author is not to be regarded as the final court of verification.

Now that we have worked out these two in principle distinct types of interpretation, the question naturally arises to which type we should assign psychoanalytic interpretations: are we dealing with hypotheses in the sense of the geologists' interpretation, or rather with constructive interpretations such as in the case of the George poem?

Let us discuss this question by using the example of a slip. Take Professor A., who as a matter of course treats his assistants in a liberal and tolerant manner. He has however a doctoral candidate, Mr. L., who somewhat strains Professor A.'s tolerance because he repeatedly violates the 'ordinary' conventions between mentor and doctoral candidate. One Tuesday afternoon the two of them arranged to meet, as they often did, to discuss the dissertation; shortly before the discussion Mr. L., who works in a clinic as a resident, called to

---

twigs/And cut for myself musical horns, it will to the hilt slash into my breast, I sink down with the setting sun./—You shall not, for it would displease me if the dark blood would cloud the dear, clear mirror of this lovely spring."

say that he could not come, he had to go instead to see the Clinic Director. Professor A. found that this was really not a proper excuse and felt a bit insulted and annoyed, especially as similar incidents had already led to trouble on a number of occasions. Nonetheless he made a new appointment for the following Tuesday.

When Mr. L. arrived the following Tuesday for the newly scheduled conference, he found the door locked: Professor A. had been unexpectedly called to a meeting in the Dean's office and had in the meantime completely forgotten the appointment with Mr. L. This slip was rather embarrassing for Professor A., and in particular it baffled him, for he almost never forgot appointments.

Let us now attempt an explanation of this slip with the help of psychoanalytic theory. Put in a highly simplified form, this theory claims that every slip is caused by an unconscious wish. This wish is formed in the situation antecedent to the slip, but the wish cannot be admitted to consciousness by the subject for moral or narcissistic reasons, and immediately becomes subject to repression.[13] The repressed wish then affects certain psychological presuppositions of our normal agency (say, our memory) in such a way that the resulting breakdown in the course of action expresses the unconscious wish. Let us apply this theory to our example: for some time Professor A. has felt irritated by Mr. L.'s behavior; he experienced the cancellation of the appointment almost as an insult, as if Mr. L. had downright 'socked him one' (all of which Professor A. is quite able to grasp in self-reflection). This gave rise to his aggressive wish to pay back Mr. L.'s behavior in the same coin. However, this wish crassly contradicted Professor A.'s

[13]The concept: "antecedent situation" of a slip, has not generally been mentioned *per se* in expositions of the theory. It is however quite central for the genetic character of psychoanalytic explanations. In this connection Freud often speaks of the "psychic situation" or the "impressions made on a person prior to the slip" (Freud, 1916/17, p. 72). In many cases the antecedent situation to which the explanation of a slip must refer reaches all the way back into childhood.

self-image as a tolerant mentor and therefore fell victim to repression. This revenge-wish asserted itself, however, in the slip in such a way that forgetting the appointment represented a wish-fulfillment in accordance with the talion principle: Mr. L. has one 'socked to him' just as Professor A. felt had been done to him.

By applying the theory to the individual case we have now explained the slip. Why, however, do we not speak simply of an 'explanation', saying instead we have *interpreted* the slip thus and so? In our opinion the element of interpretation lies in the fact that in setting it up we do indeed apply the theory of slips, but the rules for applying the individual concepts are not so precisely laid down that we can clearly and objectively decide in every case whether or not the concept should be applied. The theory claims, for example, that the unconscious wish which causes the slip has to have been formed in the antecedent situation. The antecedent situation of this slip suggests of course the formation of a revenge-wish, which then has to be repressed right away because it contradicts Professor A.'s self-image. But the indefiniteness in the concepts 'antecedent situation' or 'formation of a wish' also admits the assumption that a quite different wish could have been formed in the antecedent situation. Thus it would be conceivable, for example, that Professor A. had developed a masochistic attachment to Mr. L., which represents a threat to him; Mr. L.'s cancellation has strengthened this inclination, and the slip would be construable as the expression of an unconscious attempt to flee from further involvement.

To be sure, the first explanation fits the total situation and the special subtleties of the slip far better. What speaks in favor of the emergence of a revenge-wish is, first, the fact that Professor A. consciously felt a touch of irritation and insult when Mr. L. canceled the appointment; it did not, indeed, get as far as the formulation of a conscious wish for retribution, something which Professor A.'s highly developed ego-ideal would also not have allowed. But what speaks above all in favor of the first explanation is the almost mirror-symmetrical correspondence of Mr. L.'s cancellation and Professor A.'s slip. When Professor A. learned of the cancellation, he had (quite consciously, by the way) the feeling that Mr. L. was in a sense passing him over, preferring the Clinic Director (a nonsensical feeling, as he has to admit to himself). The slip has a completely parallel structure: the meeting in the Dean's office is so important for Professor A. that as a result he simply forgets about Mr. L.; in this there is an element of disdain, of passing over Mr. L., which makes the slip appear as the analogue of a genuine act of retribution in line with the talion principle.

But no matter how many arguments speak for the first explanation, we cannot completely exclude other explanatory possibilities. But this ambiguity of the data vis-à-vis possible explanations and therewith the necessity of having subjectively to decide in favor of one of the explanations is precisely the reason why we designate the explanation of the slip an '*interpretation*' (cf. the two essential marks of the concept of interpretation, above, p. 154).[14]

But now to which type of interpretation must we assign, for example, the interpretation of the slip? The view usually put forward in psychoanalysis is that psychoanalytic interpretations are hypotheses, i.e., true propositions which perhaps at the moment we cannot decisively verify, but which basically correspond in a clear-cut way to definite relations and situations; thus in principle they could be decisively verified, and thus have roughly the status of the geologists' interpretation.[15]

---

[14]Bernfeld, 1932, writes: Freud did not define the expression, 'interpretation', "it serves right from the start for various operations, almost as a synonym for 'explaining', 'understanding', 'guessing'" (p. 450). In my view Bernfeld here misses the special logical status of an interpretation. Nor has the later literature on the theme 'interpretation' clarified the specific semantics of interpretations. Cf. for instance Waelder, 1963, pp. 15–37.

[15]Cf. Bernfeld, 1932. Note that Bernfeld's work is still one of the best studies on the concept of interpretation in psychoanalysis. Bernfeld ex-

Now there is no mistaking the fact that in many cases one initially formulates psychoanalytic interpretations in the form of a supposition, i.e., roughly hypothetically. Further data, e.g., a dream, or more exact knowledge of the life-circumstances, or the development of the transference relationship all can give such good support to the initially merely hypothetical interpretation that we come to assert it with great certainty.

However one must keep clearly in mind that psychoanalytic interpretations can at best be supported by the furnishing of further data; they can never be conclusively verified in the way that is possible with hypothetical interpretations in the sense previously defined (cf. p. 155), e.g., the verification of a geological interpretation. This is connected with the fact that every datum which is supposed to be relied upon as support for a psychoanalytic interpretation must itself first be interpreted psychoanalytically before it can do any service in support of the interpretation. In the case of psychoanalytic interpretations there are simply no processes of verification which are independent of psychoanalytic theory (or at least none that are as yet available to us). To this extent every psychoanalytic interpretation moves in a 'hermeneutic circle.' However, we cannot at this point enter into a discussion of the exceedingly difficult, and thus far by no means solved, problem of the hermeneutical circle.[16]

---

presses, incidentally, the secret ontological presuppositon of most psychoanalysts: "It (psychoanalysis) seeks the 'correct' context and presupposes that there 'is' one such, and that it is discoverable. [Psychoanalysis] in Freud's works claims to be recognition of what is there and not interpretation." Bernfeld then continues: "Let us leave it quite open whether this goal can be reached at all, and by what methods." Too bad that Bernfeld "left it quite open," for here we have precisely the central problem of psychoanalysis from the standpoint of the philosophy of science (Bernfeld, 1932, p. 452).

[16]Occasionally one hears the opinion that this circularity is the mark of every science, and to this extent it cannot be used as an objection against psychoanalysis. For even theories in natural science move in a circle to the extent that the observational data which are supposed to

But neither are psychoanalytic interpretations hypotheses in the sense in which those literary interpretations aimed at the author's intention are hypothetical in character. We had seen that these latter can be conclusively settled by recourse to the reliable testimony of the author about his own intentions.

Now in the formation of psychoanalytic interpretations the self-reflection and utterances of the subject about himself play of course a significant role. This was also the case in the explanation of Professor A.'s slip: we learned from him, e.g., that he felt slighted and mildly annoyed when Mr. L. canceled. But, he was not, of course, conscious of the revenge-wish as the unconscious motive of his slip. Thus it is ruled out by definition that psychoanalytic interpretations could be verified by utterances of the subject about his own intentions.

Now it is striking here that psychoanalytic interpretations most resemble *constructive* interpretations in literary criticism, which indeed are also marked by the fact that the subject, the author, is not the final court of verification for the interpretation. This curious parallel suggests the thought that psychoanalytic interpretations are a variety of constructive interpetations. We saw in the case of the George poem that there are several explanatory possibilities without one of them being characterizable as *the* correct one; in itself the text is simply not bounded in a clear-cut way, it has a horizon of indefiniteness, and only in the act of interpretation does it become clearly limited to *one* sense. Now we assume that things are similar when we try to interpret Professor A.'s slip psychoanalytically: the slip, the antecedent situation, the total psychological situation, etc., etc., are just as little decisively

---

support the theory must themselves first be given a theoretical interpretation. However, one thereby overlooks the fact that usually theory and observational theory are not identical. The hermeneutical circle of psychoanalytic theory consists precisely in the fact that the observational data are interpeted with *the same* psychoanalytic theory which is supposed to be supported by these observational data.

determined as the George text, and thus they always admit of several explanations. So there simply is no real context of explanation, given in itself in reality, for one to recognize, as the geologist recognizes the true nature of the fossil footprints. It is rather the case that in the act of interpreting psychoanalytically we decide for one of the explanatory possibilities and only then do we thereby 'construct', 'constitute', 'found' a clear-cut context of explanation.

Thus every psychoanalytic interpretation contains an unavoidable element of subjective decision. However that is precisely a mark of constructive interpretations, and by no means implies (as one can never sufficiently stress) that the door is thereby opened to subjective whim. If psychoanalysis wants, in some form or other, to measure up to its claim to the status of a science, it must try to confine as far as possible this subjective factor in each of its interpretations.

A procedure meant to bring the element of subjectivity under control has long been used in psychoanalysis, namely in the form of the so-called 'counter-transference analysis', i.e., by bringing to awareness those unconscious determinants in the interpreter which lead to a distortion of his perceptual and judgmental capacities. But it is conceivable, of course, that strictly empirical procedures could be developed in order to be able properly to estimate the element of subjectivity. Here is surely one of the fields in which psychoanalysis and empirical psychology, after years of mutual distrust, could finally meet in fruitful cooperation.[17]

A comment in conclusion. If we have here asserted the parallel between psychoanalytic interpretations and constructive interpretations in literary criticism, it must nonetheless be pointed out that we have so far furnished no compelling evidence for this view.

In the case of the George poem one can with relative ease show that the text is in itself ambiguous, and that it thus

---

[17]That would be, for example, one of the tasks of consensus-research. Compare Thomä and others, 1976.

admits only of constructive interpretations. In the case of the slip it is much more difficult to demonstrate that the explananda are unavoidably ambiguous, and that psychoanalytic interpretations can in principle only have constructive character. It is of course imaginable that psychological and neurophysiological research will still one day hand us procedures that allow us decisively to verify or falsify psychoanalyic interpretations. Many things speak against such a development, but we are unable to exclude it a priori. Or are we?

Bibliography

Abel, T. 1953. "The Operation Called 'Verstehen'." In H. Feigl, and M. Brodbeck, eds., *Readings in the Philosophy of Science*. New York.

Apel, K.-O. 1973/1980. *Transformation der Philosophie*. 2 vols. Frankfurt. Selections trans. by G. Adey and D. Frisby and published as *Towards a Transformation of Philosophy*. London.

______ . 1979/1984. *Die Erklären: Verstehen-Kontroverse in transzendentalpragmatischer Sicht*. Frankfurt. Trans. as *Understanding and Explanation: A Transcendental Pragmatic Perspective* by G. Warnke. Cambridge, Mass.

Beardsley, M. 1970. *The Possibility of Criticism*. Detroit.

Bernfeld, S. 1932. "Der Begriff der 'Deutung' in der Psychoanalyse." *Zeitschrift für angewandte Psychologie* 42.

Baeumker, C. 1898. *Impossibilia des Siger von Brabant*. Münster.

Bock, C. V. 1957. "Stefan George: 'Jahrestag.'" *Castrum Peregrini* 35. Reprinted in revised form in J. Schillemeit, 1965 *Interpretationen*. Band I. *Deutsche Lyrik von Weckherlin bis Benn*. Frankfurt and Hamburg.

Brooks, C., and R. P. Warren. 1976. *Understanding Poetry*. (1st ed. 1938.) New York.

Brown, R., J. Fitzmyer, and R. Murphy. 1968. *The Jerome Bible Commentary*. Englewood Cliffs, N.J.

Buttrick, G. A., et al. 1962. *The Interpreter's Dictionary of the Bible*. New York.

Connolly, J. M. 1986. "Gadamer and the Author's Authority: A Language-Game Approach." *Journal of Aesthetics and Art Criticism* 44, no.3.

Culler, J. 1975. *Structuralist Poetics*. Ithaca, N.Y.

Davidson, D. 1980. *Essays on Actions and Events*. Oxford and New York.

______ . 1984. *Inquiries into Truth and Interpretation*. Oxford and New York.

Dilthey, W. 1927/1976. *Gesammelte Schriften*, vol. 7: *Der Aufbau der geschichtlichen Welt in den Geisteswissenschaften*. Leipzig and Berlin. In part available in English as *W. Dilthey: Selected Writings*. Ed., trans., and intro. by H. P. Rickman. Cambridge.

Dreyfus, H. 1980. "Holism and Hermeneutics." *Review of Metaphysics* 32.

Dummett, M. 1978. *Truth and Other Enigmas*. Cambridge, Mass.

———. 1979. "What Does the Appeal to Use Do for the Theory of Meaning?" In A. Margalit, ed., *Meaning and Use*. Dordrecht.

Ebeling, G. 1942,1969. *Evangelische Evangelienauslegung*. Munich, Darmstadt.

———. 1951. Die Anfaenge von Luthers Hermeneutik." *Zeitschrift fuer Theologie und Kirche* 48, pp. 172–230.

Erben, H. K. 1975. *Die Entwicklung der Lebewesen. Spielregeln der Evolution*. Munich, Zürich.

Fodor, J. 1987. *Psychosemantics*. Cambridge, Mass.

Freud, S. 1900/1965. *Die Traumdeutung*. Vienna. Trans. by J. Strachey under the title, *The Interpretation of Dreams*. New York.

———. 1916–17/1935. *Vorlesungen zur Einführung in die Psychoanalyse*. Cited from the *Studienausgabe*, Band I, 1969. Frankfurt. Trans. by Joan Riviere under the title, *A General Introduction to Psychoanalysis*. New York.

Gadamer, H. G. 1954–55. "R. Guardini, *Rilke*." *Philosophische Rundschau* 2. Reprinted in Gadamer 1967b.

———. 1958. "Zur Fragwürdigkeit des ästhetischen Bewußtseins." *Rivista di Estetica*, vol. 3, fasc. 3. Venice.

———. 1960/1975. *Wahrheit und Methode. Grundzüge einer philosophischen Hermeneutik*. Tübingen (5th ed., 1986). In English: *Truth and Method*. Trans. by G. Barden and J. Cumming. New York.

———. 1965/66. "Die Universalität des hermeneutischen Problems." *Philosophisches Jahrbuch* 73. Reprinted in Gadamer 1967a. Trans. by D. Linge in Gadamer, 1976b.

———. 1967a. *Kleine Schriften* I. Tübingen.

———. 1967b. *Kleine Schriften* II. Tübingen (2nd ed., 1979).

———. 1972/1982. "Hermeneutik als praktische Philosophie." In M. Riedel, ed., *Zur Rehabilitierung der praktischen Philosophie*, vol. 1, Freiburg. Trans. by F. G. Lawrence, in Gadamer, *Reason in the Age of Science*. Cambridge, Mass.

——— and G. Boehm, eds. 1976a. *Seminar: Philosophische Hermeneutik*. Introduction by H.-G. Gadamer. Frankfurt.

———. 1976b. *Philosophical Hermeneutics*. Trans. by D. Linge. Berkeley.

______. 1977. *Kleine Schriften* IV. Tübingen.

______. 1986. *Gesammelte Werke*, vol. I: *Wahrheit und Methode* (5th ed.) Tübingen.

George, Stefan. 1966. *Die Bücher der Hirten- und Preisgedichte, der Sagen und Sänge und der hängenden Gärten.* Düsseldorf and Munich.

Goethe, J. W. 1967. *Gedichte*. Stuttgart.

Göttner, H. 1973. *Logik der Interpretation*. Munich.

Guardini, R. 1953. *Rainer Maria Rilkes Deutung des Daseins: eine Interpretation der Duineser Elegien*. (3rd ed. 1977.) Munich.

Grünbaum, A. 1984. *The Foundations of Psychoanalysis: A Philosophical Critique*. Berkeley.

Habermas, J. 1968/1971. *Erkenntnis und Interesse*. Frankfurt.(3rd ed. 1977.) In English: *Knowledge and Human Interests*. Trans. J. Shapiro. Boston.

______. 1970a. "Der Universalitätsanspruch der Hermeneutik." In *Hermeneutik und Dialektik*. *H.-G. Gadamer zum 70. Geburtstag.* Ed. R. Bubner, K. Cramer and R. Wiehl, vol. 2. Tübingen.

______. 1970b. *Zur Logik der Sozialwissenschaften* Frankfurt. (2nd ed. 1977.)

Hahn, G. 1969. "Walther von der Vogelweide: Nemt, frowe, disen kranz (74,20)." In G. Jungbluth, ed., *Interpretationen mittelhochdeutscher Lyrik*. Bad Homburg

Hartmann, H. 1927/1964. *Die Grundlagen der Psychoanalyse*. (2nd German edition 1972.) Vienna/Stuttgart. Trans. by J. Needleman under the title "Understanding and Explanation," in H. Hartmann, *Essays in Ego Psychology*. New York.

Heidegger, M. 1927/1962. *Sein und Zeit*. (13th ed. 1976) Tübingen. Trans. as *Being and Time* by J. MacQuarrie and E. Robinson. London.

Hildebrandt, K. 1961. *Das Werk Stefan Georges*. Hamburg.

Hirsch, E. D. 1960/1967. "Objective Interpretation." *Proceedings of the Modern Language Association* 75. Cited here from the reprint, as Appendix I, in his *Validity in Interpretation*. New Haven.

______. 1965/1967. "Gadamer's *Truth and Method*." In *The Review of Metaphysics*. Reprinted as Appendix II: "Gadamer's Theory of Interpretation" in his *Validity in Interpretation*. New Haven.

Hofmannsthal, H. von. 1956. *Gesammelte Werke*. *Prosa* I. Frankfurt.

Hoy, D. 1978. *The Critical Circle*. Berkeley.

Hume, D. 1739–40. *A Treatise of Human Nature*. London. New edition, 1976, Oxford.

Jaspers, K. 1913. "Kausale und 'verständliche' Zusammenhänge zwischen Schicksal und Psychose bei dementia praecox." In *Zeitschrift fuer die ges. Neurologie und Psychiatrie* 14.

Jauss, H. R. 1982. *Toward an Aesthetic of Reception*. English trans. by T. Bahti. Minnesota.

Klein, G. S. 1976. *Psychoanalytic Theory: An Exploration of Essentials*. New York.

Kuhn, T. 1962. *The Structure of Scientific Revolutions*. Chicago.

Luther, M. 1883 ff. *Werke. Kritische Gesamtausgabe*, vol I ff. Weimar 1883 ff.

———. 1961. *Martin Luther: Selections*. Ed. J. Dillenberger. Garden City, N.Y.

MacIntyre, A. 1976. "Contexts of Interpretation." *Boston University Journal* 24.

———. 1981. *After Virtue*. Notre Dame, Ind.

Morwitz, E. 1960. *Kommentar zu dem Werk Stefan Georges*. Munich and Düsseldorf.

Morwitz, E., and C. N. Valhope. 1943. *Stefan George: Poems*. New York.

Otto, W. 1929. *Die Götter Griechenlands: Das Bild des Göttlichen im Spiegel des griechischen Geistes*. (8th ed. 1987). Frankfurt.

———. 1933. *Dionysos: Mythos und Kultus*. (3rd ed. 1960.) Frankfurt.

Palmer, R. 1969. *Hermeneutics*. Evanston, Ill.

Perrine, L. 1982. *Sound and Sense*. San Diego.

Popper, K. R. 1934/1959. *Logik der Forschung*. Vienna. (2nd ed. Tübingen 1976.) In English: *The Logic of Scientific Discovery*, trans. by the author with the assistance of J. Freed and L. Freed. London.

———. 1974. *The Philosophy of Karl Popper*. Ed. P. Schilpp. LaSalle, Ill.

Putnam, H. 1975–1983. *Philosophical Papers*. Vol. 2: *Mind, Language and Reality*. Vol. 3: *Realism and Reason*. Cambridge.

Quine, W. V. 1953. "Two Dogmas of Empiricism." In his *From a Logical Point of View*. Cambridge, Mass.

———. 1960. *Word and Object*. Cambridge, Mass.

———. 1969. *Ontological Relativity and Other Essays*. New York.

Rank, O. 1915. "Das 'Schauspiel' in 'Hamlet': Ein Beitrag zur Analyse u. zum dynamischen Verständnis der Dichtung." *Imago*, IV.

Ricoeur, P. 1981. *Hermeneutics and the Human Sciences*. Ed. J. Thompson. Cambridge.

Rilke, R. M. 1939. *Duino Elegies*. German text with English translation by J. B. Leishman and S. Spender. New York

———. 1942. *Sonnets to Orpheus*. German text with translation by W. D. H. Norton. New York.

———. 1981. *Rainer Maria Rilke: Poems 1912–1926* Selected, trans. and with an intro. by Michael Hamburger. Redding Ridge, Conn.

Rorty, R. 1979. *Philosophy and the Mirror of Nature*. Princeton.

______ . 1980. "A Reply to Dreyfus and Taylor." *Review of Metaphysics* 34.

Rothacker, E. 1948. *Logik und Systematik der Geisteswissenschaften*. Bonn.

Ryle, G. 1949. *The Concept of Mind*. London.

Schafer, R. 1976. *A New Language for Psychoanalysis*. New Haven.

Schleiermacher, F. 1959/1977. *Hermeneutik*. Ed. H. Kimmerle. (2nd ed. 1974.) Heidelberg. Trans. as *Hermeneutics: the Handwritten Manuscripts*, by James Duke and Jack Forstman. Missoula, Mont.

Schulz, H. S. 1967. *Studien zur Dichtung Stefan Georges* Heidelberg.

Sneed, J. D. 1971. *The Logical Structure of Mathematical Physics*. Dordrecht.

Specht, E. K. 1981. "Der wissenschaftstheoretische Status der Psychoanalyse. Das Problem der Traumdeutung." *Psyche* 35, Sept. 1981.

Specht, E. K., N. Erichsen and K. Schüttauf. 1987. "Bedeutung und Wahrheit von Empfindungsaussagen. Ein Diskurs zwischen Cartesianer und Wittgensteinianer." Mimeographed. Bonn.

Staiger, E. 1955. *Die Kunst der Interpretation*. Zurich. (2nd ed. 1967.)

Stegmüller, W. 1969–1973. *Probleme und Resultate der Wissenschaftstheorie und Analytischen Philosophie*. 4 vols. Berlin-Heidelberg, New York.

______ . 1970. *Aufsätze zu Kant und Wittgenstein*. Darmstadt. Translated into English in Stegmüller, 1977.

______ . 1973a. *Statistisches Schließen—Statistische Begründung—Statistische Analyse*. Berlin, Heidelberg, New York.

______ . 1973b. "Der sogenannte Zirkel des Verstehens." In K. Hübner and A. Menne, eds., *Natur und Geschichte*, Proceedings of the 10th German Congress for Philosophy, Kiel, October 1972, pp. 21–45. Hamburg. Trans. into English in Stegmüller, 1977.

______ . 1976. *The Structures and Dynamics of Theories*. Berlin, Heidelberg, New York.

______ . 1977. *Collected Papers on Epistemology, Philosophy of Science and History of Philosophy*. Trans. in part by B. Martini, partly revised by W. Wohlhueter. 2 vols. Dordrecht and Boston.

______ . 1979. *The Structuralist View of Theories. A Possible Analogue of the Bourbaki-Programme to Physical Science*. Berlin, Heidelberg, New York.

Steiner, J. 1962. *Rilkes Duineser Elegien*. Munich.

Taylor, C. 1980. "Understanding in Human Science." *Review of Metaphysics* 34.

Thomä, H., H.-J. Grünzig, H. Böckenförde, and H. Kächele. 1976. "Das Konsensusproblem in der Psychoanalyse." *Psyche* 30.

Waelder, R. 1963. *Die Grundlagen der Psychoanalyse*. Bern and Stuttgart.

Wapnewski, P. 1957. "Walthers Lied von der Traumliebe (74,20) und die deutschsprachige Pastourelle." *Euphorion* 51.

Warnke, G. 1987. *Gadamer. Hermeneutics, Tradition and Reason*. Stanford, Cal.

Weinsheimer, J. 1985. *Gadamer's Hermeneutics*. New Haven.

Weitz, M. 1964. *Hamlet and the Philosophy of Literary Interpretation*. Chicago.

Wittgenstein, L. 1953. *Philosophical Investigations*. Trans. by G. E. M. Anscombe. Oxford.

———. 1958. *The Blue and Brown Books*. Oxford.

———. 1969/1974. *Philosophische Grammatik*. Oxford. Trans. by A. J. Kenny as *Philosophical Grammar*. Oxford.

———. 1969. *On Certainty*. Oxford.

Wolf, F. A. 1807. *Darstellung der Altertumswissenschaft nach Begriff, Umfang, Zweck und Wert*. In *Museum der Altertumswissenschaft*, ed. F. A. Wolf and P. Buttmann.